D0757884

Remarriage and Your Money

Remarriage and Your Money

ONCE AGAIN, FOR RICHER OR POORER

Patricia Schiff Estess

332.024
Estess
C. 1

LITTLE, BROWN AND COMPANY

BOSTON   TORONTO   LONDON

Copyright © 1992 by Patricia Schiff Estess

All rights reserved. No part of this book may be reproduced
in any form or by any electronic or mechanical means,
including information storage and retrieval systems, without
permission in writing from the publisher, except by a reviewer
who may quote brief passages in a review.

First Edition

Library of Congress Cataloging-in-Publication Data

Estess, Patricia Schiff.
    Remarriage and your money : once again, for richer or poorer
/ Patricia Schiff Estess. — 1st ed.
        p.   cm.
    Includes bibliographical references.
    ISBN 0-316-25064-3
    1. Remarried people — Finance, Personal.   I. Title.
HG179.E85   1992
332.024 — dc20   91-16397

10   9   8   7   6   5   4   3   2   1

RRD-VA

*Published simultaneously in Canada
by Little, Brown & Company (Canada) Limited*

Printed in the United States of America

To my husband, Gene
With whom sharing means multiplying life's riches —
not dividing them

Contents

Acknowledgments

I did not write this book in a vacuum.

Almost 100 remarried couples shared portions of their lives with me. These couples are from cities and towns across the country — from Atlanta to Los Angeles, Boston to Phoenix. I chose them through recommendations but at random. All but six had been remarried for at least three years and, at the time we spoke, claimed to have found ways of dealing with the financial challenges they had faced and were continuing to confront. They were extremely honest about the difficulties of coping with their finances in the midst of divided loyalties and a new and complex relationship.

Time is a rare and precious commodity for remarrieds, yet the couples I spoke with were generous with it, both during and after the formal interviews. Although they're not identified by their real names in the book, they will recognize themselves among the pages.

The underlying truths of this book come from these remarried couples. At the time they were telling their stories, they didn't always realize that certain underlying themes would crisscross all their reflections: trust, fairness, respect, and love. Those themes permeated the talk of investments, checking accounts, financial chores, taxes, houses, and estate planning.

My thanks to the legal and financial experts who spent

time with me, sharing and checking information that would be of help to the remarried couples reading this book: Marcia Marshall, Peter Strauss, Mark Levinson, Sidney Weinman, Richard Victor, Susan Richards, Jacalyn F. Barnett, Patricia Raskob, Vicki and Russ Schultz, Marvin Strauss, Lynn Gold-Bikin, Ann Salo, Fern Topas Salka, Sandy Geller, and Murray Lennard. Their aggregate knowledge and credentials are impressive.

And to the social scientists, researchers, and students of remarriage and stepfamilies, many of whom have been quoted in this book, more thanks for helping me understand why people act the way they do: the Reverend Dick Dunn, Dr. Bernard Frankel, and Dr. Florence Kaslow. Special thanks to Linda Perlin Alperstein, a childhood friend and noted family counselor, with whom exploring ideas is always inspirational.

Two people read this manuscript before it went to the publisher: Evan Cooper, who read it with a critical eye, and my husband, Gene Estess, who read it with an uncritical eye. Both were invaluable.

My editor at Little, Brown, Fredrica Friedman, is an astute reader. I valued and appreciated her critiques and suggestions, and the work also of her associate, Rebecca MacDougall, and of my agent, Connie Clausen.

There are some people who contributed to this book without really knowing it. I can't quite put my finger on the exact words of encouragement or assistance they gave me, but I felt them with each word I wrote: my parents, Adele and Milton Schiff, and four adult children, Andrea, Peter, and Jennifer Wohl, and Noah Estess. Without them, this book wouldn't have been, couldn't have been written.

Remarriage and Your Money

Introduction

I admit to a bias. When it comes to marriages, I'll take seconds. The sharing is more caring, the trust more total, the kindness more poignant, the laughs heartier, and the pain less stabbing. We appreciate our separateness, treasure our togetherness.

Yet the start of our remarried life 15 years ago didn't promise such a tribute. To the wedding came a small assortment of relatives and just three of our eight children (ranging in ages from nine to 19). A fourth showed up after the ceremony, not because he wanted to be there, but because, being 12, he couldn't venture far from home, where the reception was being held.

The children now tell us, years later, that until that evening they had still held out hope that their biological parents would be reunited — even though deep in their hearts they knew it wouldn't happen. And they were scared about what this union would mean to them. Where would they fit in?

Gene and I chuckle now when we reflect on the evening, but few of the guests chuckled then. Although we thought we had done the necessary spadework in preparing the children for the union, we didn't realize how much more had to be done before even an acceptance of one another could grow. We were so happy we weren't really conscious of the children's casting a pall over the evening. The children eyed and stared down everyone who seemed to be enjoying the occasion. That's the reason, no doubt, that guests began their own countdown, glancing at watches, waiting for the appropriate moment to make their exit.

Other couples might have endured the day by dreaming of their honeymoon. Not us. We had canceled ours. I reasoned, unilaterally, that the children needed us around after the wedding to help them adapt. What's more, I was practical; a honeymoon would have meant beginning our married life in debt. Instead, our married life was preceded by a week of angry silence because my husband refused to share my horror over the idea of an enjoy-now-pay-later honeymoon.

(Money Lesson for Remarrieds Number One: The philosophy of the Scarlett O'Hara School of Financial Planning — I'll worry about the bill tomorrow — is not one I endorse. However, on infrequent occasions such as honeymoons, Scarlett may have been on to something.)

Finally, the evening of our wedding was over. The two of us — aglow with love for each other and for the rest of our tucked-in Brady Bunch — tumbled into bed. As we clicked off the light, we heard a knock on our bedroom door.

"Mommy, I don't feel well," the youngest child announced as she trotted in uninvited. She wasn't faking: she vomited on our bed.

So began our marriage.

No remarriage is typical, but many have common stumbling blocks. Studies have shown that money-related issues wreck remarriages as often as child-related problems. Conflicting financial values, attitudes toward and ways of managing, earning, and spending money must be addressed when "I do" is uttered for the second, third, or fourth time.

Financially, we who remarry bring down the aisle with us a train of family responsibilities much heavier than those carried by first-timers floating toward the altar tulle laden and tuxedoed. Some of us bring dependent children. Some bring adult children, some older parents. All of us bring established ways of managing the monetary aspect of these relationships, our own clearly defined money personalities, and a hodgepodge of assets, debts, plans, and dreams.

In addition to family baggage, we who remarry also carry more physical luggage: the flatware service for 12 missing three teaspoons and a salad fork; two 19-inch TVs; a dozen magazine subscriptions (including two to *Newsweek*); a cherished, almost antique chest of drawers; a Mac and an IBM computer; old LPs and a new compact disc player; one no-fee Visa, one gold Visa, one MasterCard that bills in a weird way, a Discover, three telephone, and six oil company credit cards; IRAs, rollover IRAs, and money market accounts with four mutual fund companies; 401 (k) accounts, home equity loans, three life insurance policies, overlapping medical plans, and two car-payment coupon booklets. These serve as material evidence of who we are and what we think is important.

We who remarry face different financial considerations from those we faced the first time:

• We are less well off than if we had not divorced and remarried. There's usually not as much money to go around in a second marriage as there was in a first, due to the cost of maintaining additional households. Mine wasn't the only remarriage that started on a peanut butter and jelly budget. According to the Bureau of the Census's latest report, the net worth and disposable income of remarrieds are significantly lower than those of first-marrieds.

• We are unequally endowed. Unlike many first-timers who marry younger and have had little time to accumulate wealth (or to get deeply in debt, for that matter), remarrieds often bring assets of widely disparate size to the new union. The uneven matchups can create jealousies, power plays, and insecurities.

• We are unequal before the law. Rules and customs governing financial dealings in a remarriage are complicated, confusing, and arbitrary, because they are based on guidelines designed for first-timers. State laws differ widely, and rights and responsibilities of second spouses are ill defined. For example, a stepparent's finances must be noted on a college financial aid form and taken into consideration when determining financial aid — even if the noncustodial parent, and not the stepparent, is assuming partial or total financial responsibility for college.

Despite the obstacles, remarriage can work. And work well. I know. If we had had one whit less commitment to each other, long memories, or one drop less of love, we wouldn't have made it past the first four years. Nor would we have ever received this letter on our 15th anniversary from one of the children we reared:

> It's a good thing you didn't let us sabotage your relationship like we wanted to do 15 years ago. The experiences we've had as a family have enriched us and made us better people. Some were painful. Most were wonderful. All were different. We feel your marriage enhanced us as individuals and as a family. Thank you for sharing your wonderful relationship with us and for being such great role models.

This book, intended for couples who are committed to an enduring and enriching relationship, offers guidance and information about practical financial matters.

It is written in spite of accountants who tell us, quite rightfully, that it makes "tax sense" to live together without marrying.

It is written in spite of the lawyers and financial planners who pale at the thought that people would enter into a union for the second or third time without having consulted them for a formal plan on how to divide, separate, join, and bequeath their money.

It is written for people who view marriage as a partnership of love and affection — with economics a component of the partnership. They might not feel that every dollar must be shared, but they want to be partners in the financially related aspects of their new lives.

It is written for people who are pro-marriage and pro-family, even though they may not have achieved satisfaction with the first in the past. They realize this new marriage will be different from (and definitely more complex than) an earlier one — but they think it's worth more than a stab. They're willing to take the time to act as problem solvers and creative thinkers to combat the innumerable and continuing challenges, financial and otherwise, they will face as a couple.

In the final analysis, this book is written for people who want to put money in its place. If money issues can be resolved, caringly and good-naturedly, and not become the center of ongoing disputes, then you can concentrate on the reason you married in the first place — because you love each other.

Chapter 1

In Pursuit of Trust

DID YOU KNOW . . .
- For most Americans, divorce is only a way station: 80% of men and 75% of women remarry, usually within three years.
- The United States has the highest remarriage rate in the world; more than 40% of marriages are remarriages for one or both partners.
- More than 1,400 U.S. couples form stepfamilies each day.
- If the current trends continue, by the year 2000 there will be more stepfamilies than any other kind of family in America.

By the time you find yourself approaching or in the midst of a remarriage, you have packed considerable living under your belt. Your financial experiences — from childhood, single life, first marriage, divorce or the death of your spouse, and single life again — form the basis of your opinions and attitudes about money. These beliefs become a way of life. Each person has a way of saving or not saving money, a favorite time of month to write out checks, an entrenched view of how extensively to support the children's education, a feel for appropriate gift giving, opinions on vacations, tips, and investments, at least one irrational financial fear, and much more.

Priscilla had been married for six years to a semifunctioning alcoholic who, when working, commanded a salary of between $50,000 and $75,000 as a chemical engineer. The income could have allowed them to live comfortably in Atlanta during the 1980s, but a third or more of each check was spent at bars and liquor stores or, occasionally, on repentful spending sprees that netted Priscilla dozens of roses and negligees, but no money for the mortgage. To insulate herself and her two young boys, she started stashing money from her salary in an envelope hidden in a book, and she vowed to use the cache for two things only: mortgage payments and the boys' education. When Priscilla divorced, she was stuck with $2,800 of her husband's credit card debt, which she started paying off at $20 a week. Even then she didn't reveal the existence of her stash to creditors.

When she married Sy, Priscilla continued to tuck away dollars secretly whenever she could. One day, he happened on an envelope stuffed with more than $1,900.

Because each person brings his or her individual style to money, people can't help butting up against each other when they remarry. No psychologist need tell you that if your actions were left undiscussed, resentment would build to the point that there would be no trust left in the marriage. Most people who have been through divorces know lots about resentment.

"I was devastated when I found the money," Sy says of the envelope incident. "Of course, I knew about the financial hardships Priscilla had suffered during her first marriage and when she was raising the boys alone. I didn't care that she had this cache, but the fact that she didn't tell me about it indicated she didn't trust me. How could we live this way?"

Says Priscilla: "I had been so badly burned during my first marriage. My secret account was a carryover. But I'm glad Sy found the money. Although it caused terrible grief initially, the fights we had over it served as the basis for a new understanding.

"It took months for us to peel away and discuss all the fears I had — everything from being homeless to not having any control over my life — but as we discussed them, I felt better. Sy is really a wonderful person. He listened, he empathized, he shared with me stories in his life that were parallel or that revealed his own financial fears. And in the final analysis, he did something I never could have expected, nor had I even thought about. He paid off the remaining $1,800 debt I had inherited from my first husband. While he was writing out the check, I sat at the kitchen table and cried with joy and with love for him."

Money and Your Former Life

Remarriages — by virtue of their "re" status — mean that something has gone wrong the first time. If you lost a spouse through death, you might feel cautious, protective, guilty for being happy. If you have gone through a divorce, you might bring a sense of distrust, guilt, or illusion to this new relationship. Any of these emotions can affect your present finances. An adversarial attitude toward money developed in a divorce proceeding can spill over into the new marriage. Guilt over the breakup of a first marriage can lead to excessive generosity toward the first family, to the financial detriment of the second. More subtle, but just as debilitating, may be the hope that this marriage will be everything the first was not, blinding you to the need to address practical monetary concerns.

Because money has such powerful emotional overtones in a remarriage, and because there is no single type of remarried family (the variations are endless), there are no absolute or simple solutions. What's best is what you as a couple can agree on. But that agreement takes time and talk.

While it's nonsense to assume that if you talk about something before a remarriage you'll be able to work it out by the time the rings get slipped on, it is true that you and your partner can encourage the growth of trust by talking about obvious financial differences as soon as the relationship moves into a serious stage.

Before remarriage (and nonstop throughout it, of course), it's essential to be open and honest about your financial situation. Financial information — whether it's yours, mine, or ours — must always be shared. Putting down on paper the facts and figures of your assets, liabilities, income, expenditures, and responsibilities is easier than discussing styles, attitudes, and values. And just seeing those numbers on paper elicits a feeling of trust.

Numbers also serve as the basis for ongoing discussions. What lies behind them? While each of us secretly wishes we were marrying for the first time (thus eliminating the former mates and alliances that are unfamiliar and wrenching to this new relationship), we realize that the soon-to-be-spouse is what he or she is because of the experiences that came before. Former husbands and wives are just that: former. And children from a former marriage are always children, even in cases where they are estranged. There is no such thing as "ex" in a remarriage. You can't x "formers" out of your life, like them or not. The Jewish proverb "When two divorced people marry, four get into bed" survived because it's uncomfortably true. Whether through alimony, support, or everyday existence, former spouses and their relatives constantly influence and intrude on the newly married couple's lives — frequently financially.

The numbers prove it. "He still has to make payments on a Mercedes which his former wife's new husband drives," one irate second wife says about her executive husband, who was out of work due to a corporate merger.

Talking about the numbers uncovers more than a financial picture. It provides a mirror of who you are and what's happening inside of you.

Muses one second husband, half-resentfully and half-admiringly, about his new wife's sense of loyalty: "There's $50 a month in our budget for her former husband's elderly aunt. She won't cut it out because this was a woman who helped her out financially and emotionally during her divorce. That $50 would allow us a couple of much-needed long weekends during the year, but . . ."

Stages of Trust

Anita and Edward Metzen (she the executive director of the American Council on Consumer Interests, and he a professor and chair of the Department of Family Economics and Management at the University of Missouri), themselves remarried, have defined five money stages most remarrieds go through.

1. *The Rose-Colored-Glasses Stage.* In those romantic first moments, money talk seems crass or unimportant because either the strength of love will handle everything (naïveté), or there will be no money conflicts (ignorance).

2. *The Don't-Rock-the-Boat Stage.* Feelings of resentment or anger surface. Frequently such thoughts as "Why should I resent his paying alimony? I knew about it before we got married" or "I can't stand her cheapness when it comes to gift giving. I like to give the best" aren't voiced for fear that any stress would put too much pressure on the fragile, new union.

In his first marriage, John had complete control over the finances. "I'm the type who, when I saw what I thought was a good investment, borrowed money to take advantage of it," he said three years into his marriage.

"I couldn't believe he would make these kinds of decisions without even speaking to me about it," said Judy, John's second wife. "But I hesitated to say anything, because he wasn't signing my name to the loan."

3. *The Lay-It-on-the-Table Stage.* Couples painfully hear and express their concerns with each other, feeling it's okay

to be honest with each other, to argue about spending priorities, to speak candidly about their feelings, frustrations, and fears surrounding their finances. A foundation of trust is being laid, albeit roughly.

"I finally couldn't stand it anymore. After all, I was scrimping to contribute money to my 401(k) plan at work so we'd have money for retirement, and he was borrowing money for investments — which might or might not pay off," Judy said. "I told him I couldn't stand not being part of investment decisions."

"I was surprised and more than a little annoyed at first," John admitted. "That's the way I've always operated. It was as if she didn't trust my judgment."

4. *The Getting-It-Together Stage.* The couple has by now arrived at a mutually agreed-upon lifestyle and has established an effective method of handling finances and making financial decisions. It doesn't necessarily mean that they've commingled funds, just that they have *agreed* on contributions — both monetary contributions and contributions of time — and that they have a system in place for managing both jointly owned and separately owned property.

"Judy's a good money handler, and I understand her need to be consulted before I make an investment, so that's how we handle this now," John said. "But," Judy added, "we have separate accounts and John's debt and consequent investment must be taken care of from his account. I don't try to dissuade him from the investment, unless I think it's a real rotten idea, because he's astute in this area. Though this type of money management still makes me uncomfortable, at least I don't have to see interest payments on a loan being written out each month."

5. *The Achieving-Stability Stage.* The couple really feels in control of finances. Despite the ultimate instability of anyone's financial position, they now feel comfortable adjusting their goals or spending patterns as circumstances require.

Their perspectives are integrated. They can handle change.

"This year John had cancer surgery," says Judy, now five years into the marriage. "For ease of managing money, we decided to join our accounts. We talk about everything now, but I'm handling all the money for a while. John trusts that I'll take care of things as best as I can. We're much more conservative now because, quite frankly, we don't know what the future holds."

Entrenched Money Styles

By the time a man and woman remarry, their culture, experience, personal chemistry, and individual thinking have had time to mix and harden. They are fairly well defined people who, as a couple, don't share a thick middle ground. And that gives them a wide playing field for conflict. For a remarriage to work, the middle ground, defined by Patricia L. Papernow, Ph.D. and codirector of the Charles River Gestalt Center in Newtonville, Massachusetts, as "an area of shared experience, shared values, and easy cooperative functioning, created over time," must broaden.

Financial differences that turn on values, those principles that guide decisions, are the most difficult to resolve. Values stem from childhood and are expressed in political, religious, and social orientation. Even without a conscious determination, they pilot people's actions as parents, spouses, employees and employers, community members, relatives, and friends.

If two people have significantly different definitions of honesty, for example, they will have problems trusting one another. Suppose a husband is freewheeling with his expense account, charging everything — the family's sports-event attendance, expensive dinners out, and much, much more — to the company, while his wife seethes, self-righteous about the abuse, and refuses to go out with him if he continues. It's a bad sign for the marriage.

And there are even wider schisms. I knew of one New York man who, in an effort to raise capital for a business, deliberately withheld information about his partners (two men who had served jail terms for grand larceny) from his wife's relatives when he asked them to invest in the deal. The projected profits, he reasoned, were more important than full disclosure. When she discovered the truth, his wife disagreed — so strongly that within a few months she instituted divorce proceedings.

Clearly, remarrieds will not have identical value systems, but each of their highest priorities should be mesh-able, so there's a possibility of planning and living a life together.

Values are different from styles. Values are the conscious or unconscious beliefs you feel in your gut. Styles are the expressions of those values. You both might value financial security, but where one of you views it as owning your home mortgage-free another might see it as having enough money saved or invested not to threaten your lifestyle if you decide to take a lower-paying job doing something you really love.

Styles are influenced by many factors — your personality and your confidence level being two important ones. Introverts and extroverts might contribute the same $5,000 to the American Cancer Society each year, but one might do it anonymously and the other might want to be listed in all the charity's literature.

How you handle money also has to do with your confidence in your ability to earn it. One banker put it this way: "If I hadn't been let go twice in the past two years as a result of all these damn layoffs, I'd be a lot less skittish about dipping into our savings to buy a new car." His wife, who is a nurse and never lacking for work, is much less concerned about the expenditure. "You'll get another job soon and you'll need the car. So why not buy it now since they're offering a good deal?" she argues with assurance.

Women who make their first major foray into the workplace immediately after a divorce frequently feel and act as if they're one step away from poverty, despite the fact they might have substantial assets or be earning an impressive salary. Their confidence as money makers and managers has not yet developed. Often they drag that lack of confidence and its coexisting lifestyle into a new marriage.

Much is made about differences in money styles. Certainly many marital arguments revolve around them. You know the scenarios. She never seems to worry about money; he comparison shops tomatoes. She constantly forgets to enter checks she wrote in the checkbook; he's a fanatic about reconciling the bank statement. He wants to give his children everything he didn't have as a child; she feels her children ought to be responsible for earning their spending money.

We were a screaming example of how the differences can affect a relationship. My husband, Gene, had a considerable support commitment and no savings. A year before we were married he returned to Wall Street (after a two-year hiatus). It was going to take time to build up a client list again. We both knew that. In the first year of our marriage even our modest lifestyle meant we were living way beyond our joint incomes and deep into my limited savings. Our entertainment budget was confined to haunting flea markets on weekends and picking up old medicinal tin containers for Gene's collection. Though I loved the new activity, I lived in terror that Gene would stumble on a "find" and plunk down $200, pushing us still further into my savings. Initially, I'd balk at his purchases, commenting on "the condition" of the tin, or find some other reason why he shouldn't buy it. If he succumbed to my resistance, he'd sulk and insist on going home immediately. If he did buy it, I'd pick a fight.

Do markedly different styles doom a remarriage to nagging, squabbles, resentments, down-and-dirty fights? No. Conflicts in style create problems because of the way they're handled, not because they exist. In their in-depth research on couple relationships published in *American Couples*, Drs. Philip Blumstein and Pepper Schwartz concluded that "the mere fact that a couple has very different ideas about how to spend money does not necessarily mean they have more conflict. If, however [and this is especially important], in addition to having different views, at least one partner feels he or she cannot exert any control over spending, then we often observe anger and frustration."

Handled properly, different styles give the couple a new sense of closeness and confidence they can navigate other differences because they've reached a solution together. Conflict also prevents boredom and leads to resolutions that bring new dimension and experience to both husband and wife.

While neither Gene nor I wanted to wind up in debt, for example, we had very different thresholds of comfort with our situation. Gene was confident he'd be financially successful again. I was wary and felt threatened. Eventually our accusations led to an expression of the real pressures each was feeling: Gene, trapped in a financial half nelson; I, fearful we would further tip our already tilted financial situation. But we've always respected each other's feelings, so once we understood the fears and needs, we were able to work out a solution. We set a dollar limit on our monthly flea-market jaunts. We decided to buy some of the household items we needed at the markets — a bedspread, a lamp, a spatula — so we could experience the fun of hunting even though we were shopping for necessities. And Gene suggested I start collecting the Depression glass water goblets I always admired. He was more than happy to suspend tin purchases to see the joy I got from buying one $5–8 glass each outing. It was a solution that worked for us.

Now, 15 years later, Gene and I exchange sly smiles when people comment on my wonderful goblet collection and his fabulous medicinal tins. They could probably guess the problems and then the fun we had finding these love objects, but little do they know that those 25 glasses, costing a total of less than $200, saved us thousands on marriage counseling. Nor could they know that the goblet resolution was the first of many creative problem-solving exercises we have had to go through because we have such different money styles. With each one, we've increased our closeness and our trust both in each other individually and as a team.

Spouses Can Alter Styles

One spouse's distinct money style frequently has a definite effect on the other's. It can push people to the right or left of themselves.

Bob, a Boston entrepreneur, tells how his first wife spent money before he earned it. Nothing was too good for her or the children. The Elsa Perretti jewelry was "a must"; the children not going to summer camp was unheard of. He constantly found himself in the position of spoiler. "I was the one who told my daughter she couldn't have the diamond studs she wanted for her 12th birthday. I was the one who screamed about department store bills as they came in each month. I didn't like being the ogre, but I always felt I had to balance my former wife's unbridled spending."

When Bob married Roberta, he took on a different persona — one of benefactor. He finds himself prodding Roberta to buy a new dress or urging her to get the next-to-best room at a resort rather than the cheapest. "I'm now on the other end of the seesaw," he says.

"I have had to be very careful with money because I had so little when I was raising my children," says Roberta, who was a single parent for thirteen years. "I don't like to waste money. I don't care if it's Bob's or mine."

Bob claims he's much more comfortable in this new position and Roberta says that even though she still is frugal, she's learning to loosen up and enjoy herself more. Though the shift in attitudes has not been dramatic, it has occurred. And both feel better about it. Clearly people can relax and enjoy themselves more when they're not too far left nor too far right of their gravitational center.

Fairness Counts . . . but Not for Everything

Marriage is marriage, whether it's a first marriage or a remarriage. Inherent in its meaning is financial fairness. To the extent fairness can be maintained, it should be, because it's a building block for trust.

Yet it's almost impossible to even out the financial ground. One of you might sell your house for five times its purchase price while the other barely broke even. One of you might have been born to rich parents and one of you wasn't. One of you might have invested $80,000 for a child's college education while the parent of the other child (who's a far better student) may have saved nothing. Are any of these situations fair?

While we can try, eliminating the situations that foil fairness is like plucking weeds from the garden. You clear the area of choking growths, but you don't assure yourself of flowering plants — or even that you're rid of weeds forever. Part of the problem is that you don't have ultimate control over financial fairness. So the question is, If establishing financial fairness is so difficult, is the struggle worth the effort?

In the end, the answer is equivocal. For certain, attempt to be fair. But where fairness isn't possible, work to find practical solutions and move on with life. Endeavoring to put fairness in terms of dollars and cents or participation, for example, may not be a productive way to build trust. You might have to find another way, such as accepting that there are certain financial situations that can't be balanced.

Money Talk: An Aphrodisiac

"Although it's more than twenty years ahead of us, we've been talking a lot about retirement recently," Derek says. "I have fond

memories of Oregon from when I worked there during one of my college summers. I've always thought that's where I'd like to retire. I thought it was important for Susie to see what I was dreaming of. She thought so too. We really didn't have the money to vacation in style because I was paying my boys' college tuitions, but this past summer we used frequent-flyer tickets, took our daughter Christen (age two), and stayed with my sister. It worked out fabulously. Susie fell in love with the land too. Now there's something else we have in common, something we can look forward to and save for together.''

There's romance in dreaming together. Hot air ballooning in France, seeing a child graduate, or buying a home of your own are dreams that require planning — financial planning.

Remarried couples who don't use money talk to increase romance are missing out on the aphrodisiac of our time.

Money talk is good pillow talk even when the intimacy achieved is not romantic. In times of financial crisis, people who have communicated their money values, attitudes, and feelings are better able to support each other — emotionally and practically — than those who don't know each other as well. Quite simply, they trust each other more.

Trust . . . and a Leap of Faith

Seasoned by caring, communicating, laughter, shared experience, effort, problems, and problem solving, a committed remarriage settles into a trusting relationship, one in which you feel safe. Your partner may not always handle money to your liking, but you don't feel threatened that the actions are meant to harm you. Researchers say it can take as many as seven years for this to occur, if you don't get mired in one of remarriage's developmental stages. Trust builds slowly, through a series of minor events, such as saving together to buy a home, giving a stepchild some money for college, transferring a piece of property to a new spouse, figuring out ways to merge financial styles. People usually don't have any idea when the trust has rooted.

For others, the moment of trust is seared in memory as an act of faith.

Cathy brought a three-year-old to this new union and Frank had a 10-year-old from a former marriage. ''Three years into our marriage Frank approached me with the idea that he'd like to adopt my daughter,'' Cathy says. (Her first husband had disappeared shortly after their baby was born and when she was able to track him down was amenable to the idea of Frank's adoption.)

''I'll never forget the scene in the lawyer's office just before Frank signed the papers. The lawyer said, 'Frank, I want you to understand you don't have to do this. More than that, understand that if your marriage to Cathy doesn't work out, you're financially responsible for this child. I'm going to leave you alone for a few minutes to think about that.'

''Frank looked at me, looked at the lawyer, then said, 'I've thought about it. This is what I want.'

''I'd known for some time that I loved Frank. But from that moment on, I knew he was someone I could always count on,'' says Cathy as a tear slides down her cheek.

Chapter 2

Talk to Me

DID YOU KNOW ...

- Most remarrieds who are reluctant to talk about money say that financial problems contributed to a prior divorce.

"Whenever Laurie started talking about her concern that we didn't have enough money for this or that, I tightened up," Greg, *a 41-year-old Moline, Illinois, retailer, says. "It felt like a grade-B movie flashback to my former marriage when all my first wife ever did was criticize me for not earning enough, for being a constant failure — no matter how hard I worked or how much I earned. So when Laurie voiced concern over money, it had a perverse effect on me. I just clammed up and wanted to go out and spend irresponsibly. Often I did. That just accelerated her panic, of course."*

Says Laurie: "Since my motive in discussing money was not to belittle Greg in any way, but to plan as a couple how we should manage what we had, I didn't realize that I was evoking images of 'the queen of evil' or sounding like her, God forbid. Frankly, until he explained it — and that didn't come for maybe eight or ten months into the marriage — it annoyed the hell out of me that he wouldn't even talk about money matters and that he seemed to enjoy making me crazier about the subject than I already was."

Talk is a must.

Talking about money works on many levels.

At different times in a relationship — at different times during the day — money talk can fuel conflict, can be the access route by which two people learn more about each other, or can be the stuff of dreams. Sometimes it can be all three at the same time.

Making allies of time and talk so they become planks of a wide middle ground of trust — the trust that serves as the basis for money agreement rather than conflict — is no simple task. It's difficult for a person who has been living alone and quite comfortable with independence. It's difficult for someone fresh out of a hostile divorce.

Major impediments to the free flow of rational discussion are the subjects that provoke intense visceral reactions — your financial hot buttons.

Hot Buttons

Hot buttons flood people with anxiety triggered by feelings of insignificance, mistrust, anger, jealousy, guilt, shame, or sadness. The buttons themselves aren't universally dangerous. Consider some of the hot buttons encountered in a survey. Some may send sparks flying in you, too, but chances are most will leave you unmoved and wondering why they're cause for anyone's concern.

A single joint checking account

"I don't want his alimony check written from our account. Why should I foot the bill for his mistake?"

Separate checking accounts

"He loved his first wife more than he does me. He held everything jointly with her."

Former wife is going to Europe

"That bitch. She doesn't stop suing me for more money and now she's off on a fancy vacation."

Former spouse's new wife is wealthy

"He's living in a $500,000 home overlooking Lake Michigan. Why is he such a cheap bastard when it comes to our kids?"

His children go to camp

"We're not going anywhere. His kids come before us."

Her daughter needs braces

"It frosts me that her father, who's very well off, won't pay for this because it isn't included in his separation agreement and I, her stepfather, will wind up footing the bill."

She pays for groceries, going out, baby-sitter; he pays the mortgage

"He always says that he 'keeps the roof over my head.' That's what my father kept threatening my mother with when she said she wanted a divorce."

Defusing Hot Buttons

Finding a way to defuse hot buttons is essential if you ever want productive talk on an explosive subject. One way, suggested by Linda Perlin Alperstein, a family therapist in San Francisco, is to open the conversation with a "time-setter": "You know, the subject of Johnny's braces has been on my mind. When would be a good time for us to talk about it?" Once you set a time, Alperstein says, you know you have gotten permission from your partner that it's okay to talk about this subject. Agreement to talk may be the only agreement you'll have at the moment, but at least it's a start.

Even more effective in cooling down hot tempers is what Alperstein calls the "If I Got You Correctly" exercise. "It's slow and it's tedious because it interferes with the way people normally fight. And it's hard work. But it is effective in defusing emotions and forcing people to listen to each other," she says.

It works this way.

1. You make a statement.
2. Before your partner can respond, he or she must rephrase what you said: "If I got you correctly, you are pissed off that you are being asked to foot the bill for Johnny's braces."
3. If the assessment is right, your partner proceeds with a response.
4. If the assessment is wrong (and only you can judge that), you have to rephrase what you said (without going into a tirade) and your partner tries the "If I got you correctly" again.
5. If your partner assesses your feelings correctly, then it's his (or her) turn to respond.
6. You have to do an "If I got you correctly" rephrasing of your partner's statement.
7. The process repeats itself.

"There are two key elements in this exercise," Alperstein explains. "The first is that you *don't have to agree*, but you *do have to understand* what your partner is saying. The second is that *understanding, by itself, can be a healer*. People don't have to be agreed with all the time, but they do need to be understood."

A Case for "If I Got You Correctly"

Knowing oneself doesn't assure change . . . or harmony. Consider June, a 49-year-old Rockville, Illinois, woman, who manages the home, her 17-year-old son (but not her husband John's children), and the couple's social life.

"My father died when I was seven. Though my mother didn't have to be conservative with money, she was . . . and I felt very deprived. I've explored this feeling of deprivation at length with my therapist and I know that's why I married my first husband. He was very rich and would take care of me financially. With John [her second husband of three months] I feel very loved. But I know myself. I wouldn't be happy with someone who didn't have money. I need to be taken care of. I don't want to be poor."

June has made her position clear to John. "He knew before he married me how I felt, so he can't have complaints now." But he does.

"I understand June," John says, though he wouldn't discuss his feelings in front of her. "And I don't mind being the provider. I, too, was brought up feeling that that was my responsibility. But in my business [he's a real estate deal maker] there's always the possibility that I'll have a really bad year. I'm having one right now. Even when June listens to me talk about business, I don't get the feeling she understands or wants to hear me. And it's not because she isn't capable. She's very capable. That hurts me. In addition to worrying that I might not be able to support her in the style we'd both like, I'm afraid she'll just take off and leave me the way my first wife did."

If "I got them correctly," June is panicked about the possibility of not having enough money, and neither she nor John is hearing the pain of abandonment each associates with money.

Knowing the Facts

For purposes of communication, knowledge of the actual (as opposed to the imagined) financial facts often can defuse the emotional flares associated with money.

John and June's money problems aren't severe. As John explained it, they have a substantial reserve, upward of one million dollars in stock, and three pieces of property — their luxury condo and two rental properties that pay for themselves and throw off a reasonable profit. His income has dropped, to be sure; it is down to $175,000 this year (compared to $400,000 plus for each of the past three years), but they certainly aren't starving. They don't really have to cut back on their expenses, though it would make him feel better if they did. "The flower bills kill me. I know it's a small thing in the scheme of things, but I can't believe we spend $90 a week on flowers in the house. I've asked June not to do this anymore, but she insists — saying she's using her money, so why should I care. I wish she used her money for groceries when her son comes home from boarding school."

If John were to lay out what they had, what they were bringing in, what they were spending, and if June could listen to John's recitation of the facts and be able to tolerate the idea that he, too, needs time to worry, chances are she wouldn't feel so threatened when he complains about business. "I'm not going to fink out on my responsibility to support her," John says. "What I need is someone I can trust to complain to, to air my frustration with."

Sharing financial information is fundamental to a good marriage — even if it causes friction. The wife who gives her son $5,000 from her own account as a down payment for a car may be in for a "that-kid-doesn't-deserve-it" tirade from her husband, who doesn't share her largess. But the damage to the relationship from this conflict isn't as corrosive as it would be if her husband uncovered the secret gift later. It's not the data itself that is so important; it's the act of sharing confidentialities that strengthens the bonds of love. Deep secrets between spouses can destroy marriages.

Whether before or during a remarriage, couples will feel more comfortable with finances if they share information about income, expenses, and assets — openly and regularly.

A "More Talk, Less Fight" Communications Plan

"It sounds ridiculous, I know, but we have a regularly scheduled finance meeting on Sunday afternoon — after the televising of whatever the major game of the season is, naturally — and we talk about anything and everything dealing with our money," says Brenda, 51, a high school social studies teacher in Miami. "In the early stages of our marriage, we talked about my anger over how much Barry gave his boys, how unfair that was to my children; why I had a need to ask him before I bought anything, and how he resented that; about our wills. Then, as our marriage rooted, we did more planning and less arguing. Now, 16 years later, we are doing some estate planning, figuring out how to reduce insurance costs. Sometimes we just use this regularly scheduled finance time to write out checks."

For a "more talk, less fight" communication process designed to increase trust:

Set a specified time and place to discuss money matters. The time should be convenient and the setting relaxed (not in bed, though, unless your talk is romantic — like planning a trip to Hawaii). Take a walk or sprawl out on the lawn if you have serious grievances to discuss. Use the dining-room table if you need to spread out the checkbooks, budgets, or investment statements — but sit on the same side of the table and not across from each other in a confrontational position. Don't pick a spot that weighs in someone's favor (like a room with one comfortable chair, not two) or anywhere that one of you feels insecure or out of place (like a study used by only one of you).

Set ground rules for your money talks. Whether at scheduled or spontaneous money talks, focus on what you're feeling. "I'm angry because your children get everything they ask for" is a more productive springboard for discussion and less threatening to your spouse than "Your children are spoiled brats." If one lapses into accusations, make it fair game for the other to ask for a rephrasing of the statement.

Set a time limit on the conversation and don't allow it to drone on. And take care that the subject doesn't creep in at unexpected times. "What I can't stand," says Aaron, a San

Francisco public works administrator, "is when we see someone buying or wearing something expensive and Pearl points out how excessive the purchase is. I have a tendency to overspend and I know she's leveling her remarks at me, even if she doesn't say so directly — though most of the time she makes the connection."

Because money sometimes is a cover for other issues, it's easy to go from one subject (like anger over having to use some of one's own earnings to pay for a stepchild's education) to another (being afraid you won't have enough money to finance the education of the child you had together). When you use one issue to delve into the underlying concern, that's productive. When you get sidetracked and jump from one money issue (car insurance) to another (gifts) in the same discussion, that's unproductive.

Base your talks on facts. Having the facts in front of you helps to diffuse the anxieties and often helps a couple find a solution to a money problem.

"I used to worry — and worry Suzanne — so much about finances, that we'd wind up screaming about it in some crazy frenzied state," says Noel, 42, manager of marketing support for an Illinois insurance company. "I was frantic about how I was going to put my three children and our two through college, about how we could afford to take a vacation, about how we were ever going to amass enough money to retire. Then, several years ago, I bought a $16 calculator that does present and future value analysis. It has done more for our marriage than any other purchase. I found out that even at an annual 5 percent inflation rate, we'd still have enough for retirement. Knowing that has helped relieve some of my pressure. We feel comfortable enough about our future that we took out a home equity loan to pay for my kids' schooling. Assuming we remain in good health, we'll be able to repay it easily in a few years. This calculator has brought a certain amount of peace to our lives."

Communicate creatively. Realizing that each of you has different hot buttons, try not to aim for them. Seek an oblique approach instead.

Remarried couples have so many real issues to discuss, it may seem silly to drop everything to talk about a bunch of test questions posed in a book or magazine or to develop lists about spending priorities, for example. But it's the very fact that these exercises aren't directly related to your life that makes them valuable and fun — and the basis for interesting planning.

Think, for example, of how you envision yourselves financially five years from now, assuming there is no major collapse of the economy or your personal financial situation.

Ask yourselves what money meant to your parents and to your former spouse. Was it meant to be saved, to be used for fun, for education, for the children, for charity? How did these people's ideas of money influence your life?

Sharing these visions and experiences helps to explain who you are and why.

"I'm a very emotional arguer," says Ilana, a Los Angeles mother of two toddlers. "I cry and become irrational. Then Paul says in a very modulated tone, 'There's no reason to yell' and it just gets me crazier. So I write him letters. They allow me to think through my anger and channel it into an explanation Paul would understand. When he comes home and there's a letter on his pillow, Paul knows there's something important we have to talk about."

If members of a debating team, professional salespeople, and super-articulate men and women practice how they're going to say something, why shouldn't you? Don't hesitate to practice in front of a mirror or to memorize opening lines.

Communicate personally. Whatever the money concern, realize you're in a marriage together. Look at and talk directly to each other. Don't wait until your mother comes over to grouse about your spouse's spending habits. Talking through another person is a trust-buster and rightly inflames emotions.

When looking at your finances and brainstorming for solutions, use "we" instead of "I" or "you." In a remarriage, each of you has added obligations — financial and emotional — but you're still a couple. As such, you must work out challenges together.

To find out exactly where each of you stands and how far apart you are, you might give each other a chance to voice your "druthers."

HE: "If I had my druthers, we'd track down Susie's father — no matter where he is — and sue him not only for back child support but for every other thing he said he'd pay for but never did."

SHE: "If I had my druthers, we'd forget he ever existed."

Anger with a former spouse has a way of spilling over into the next marriage. Fight the anger, not the new spouse. True, your first wife had an entitlement mentality that was infuriating and costly. But just because your present wife is excited about buying a new dress doesn't mean you have to tense up and start an argument — fearing a similar attitude. And if your first husband stalked around the house every hour shutting off lights in order to save on electricity costs, don't label your present husband cheap merely because he turns off lights when he leaves a room.

Don't be afraid to disagree. As a married couple, you've created a safe place (institution, if you will) to fight about money — as long as you fight fairly. "The ideology of marriage helps a couple absorb a great deal without collapsing. Thus permanence and security permit greater conflict among married couples," say Drs. Philip Blumstein and Pepper Schwartz in *American Couples*.

Realize there are some gender differences. Men and women traditionally feel and act differently about money. Money represents security and autonomy to women; identity and power to men. To test whether you fall into the majority, discuss with one another what each of you means when you say "financial security."

Valuable communication gets lost, says Victoria Felton-Collins, author of the book *Couples and Money*, because of cross-gender translation. When men joke about money, women interpret it as not caring about them or the problem. When men advise, women think they are being patronized. When women confide a problem, men feel like they are being burdened with unnecessary information. When women confront, men interpret it as nagging.

These are generalizations, of course. But examine your own discussions. Do they fall into these patterns?

Exacerbating the cultural and traditional money differences between the sexes are the differences in how men and women perceive the effects of their divorces. Women usually feel they were burned; men usually feel they were hung out to dry. While there are cases in which the man truly wound up the financial loser in a divorce, that isn't the general rule, statistically. (In fact, on average, the standard of living for a woman with custody of children drops significantly after a divorce and a man's increases significantly.)

Realize there might be one or two financial areas where you feel there can be no compromise. Allow your spouse the same latitude. Everyone has some "musts" when it comes to money. And once the "musts" have been voiced, they must be respected (even if they're viewed as quirks or verging on insanity). One "must" could be as simple as "I can't bear the idea of losing all our money in a bank failure. I want some within touching range." (In this case, you might have to stash some cash in the time-honored safe between the box spring and mattress.) Or a "must" can be complex. "Because the cancer I had two years ago would be considered a preexisting medical condition when it comes to insurance coverage, I won't risk moving so far away that I couldn't work for this company any longer. It might jeopardize my coverage," says a Roanoke, Virginia, woman contemplating remarriage to a Boston engineer. Her feelings are unequivocal; she would resent any attempt to talk her out of them.

Agree to disagree or postpone a decision. There are money solutions that you can't (or don't want to) resolve in a session or a series of discussions. Sometimes you're too set in your ways; sometimes you don't trust enough. The passage of time sometimes resolves conflicts; so do changes in circumstances.

"I wanted him to take on some financial responsibility for my son's college education," Theresa says of her third husband, who had provided for his own children's schooling but wasn't anxious to be saddled with another tuition. "From the first week of our marriage, we battled. I insisted it was unfair that the children have different amounts available to them — especially considering my son was a more diligent student. He felt it was my first husband's responsibility, even though the bum said he wouldn't do it. But since we were three years away from my son's freshman year, I backed off for a while." Eight months later, Theresa's current father-in-law died and left her husband a small inheritance. "Even before the probate, Richard came to me and said, 'Don't worry about schooling. If his bastard father won't pony up, I'll pay for it.' "

Collaborate on a settlement. Think of yourselves as partners in a head-to-head search for a fair agreement that will satisfy you both. Negotiating the settlement is a four-point process.

1. Separate the person from the problem. The problem isn't him or his children. The problem is that you feel jealous because he constantly gives his children gifts and you get nothing.

2. Focus on interests, not positions. Interests are what motivate us. They are the silent movers behind our positions. His position might be "I see my children so infrequently; I want to give them things." Your position is "We can't afford it." But if you allow each other to blow off steam and acknowledge and understand one another's emotions, then you can focus on what's behind the positions. Ask why. In this case, the interests — "It's important that my children feel loved" and "It's important that I feel loved" — are not necessarily in opposition.

Then ask yourself what step you could take toward your partner's point of view. Even if it's a tiny step — "I'd like you to include me as the gift-giver once in a while" — it says you're agreeing to shift your position somewhat and concentrate on your partner's interest. He responds with "Perhaps we can limit how much we'll spend when they come to visit." And so on toward a compromise.

3. Come up with a variety of possibilities before deciding what to do. There is never one right solution — especially in remarriages, where textbook solutions don't exist. Try these techniques for brainstorming:

- put yourself in your spouse's shoes
- ask his or her advice on how to deal with the situation
- adopt a no-criticism rule when a solution is offered
- use one idea to generate another
- dovetail differing interests

4. Base your decision on some objective criteria. How much money is available for gift giving — to children and to

each other? What are other ways to show love? What have other couples done in a similar situation?

What Happens to the Stuff That Doesn't Get Said?

Fear of fighting, of uncovering sharp, irreconcilable differences, prevents some people from talking about what's on their minds. Doris, a Detroit teacher, has no idea of whether or not her husband of five years has a will, or if he does, what's in it. "I'm afraid to ask him," she says. "What if he has left his children everything and me nothing? I'd be so hurt. And I don't know how to broach the subject. I don't like to talk of death nor do I want to sound like I'm interested in his money."

Here is a communication gap that is eroding trust and could filter down to become a major financial problem. Even though Doris, as a spouse, is protected from being disinherited under the laws of the state, she doesn't know what she can expect, financially, if her husband dies. At this point, she'd do well to broach the subject not from the angle of wills and death but by admitting to her husband that she's worried about her reticence to share something that has been on her mind.

When spouses refuse to address financial issues or pretend they don't exist, when they cloud financial issues or avoid dealing with the real issues (Is the fight over how much money he spends on his visiting children grounded in jealousy or money?), trust erodes — and with it the marriage.

Many people well up with resentment over financial matters but don't know themselves well enough to realize what is behind this feeling. Prodding feelings with "whys" and exploring background and experience — either together or with the help of a professional — can break the communication logjam.

Who Can Help?

Feeling nobody else has ever faced the problems of re-marriage that you face is natural. Yet despite the uniqueness of your situation, there are identifiable patterns in remarriage. And talking to others about them is valuable because once you understand that you're not alone and that blame lies not with your spouse or the children, you can begin to address the complexities of remarriage. Also, if your emotions are so close to the surface that you can't talk rationally to your spouse about them, seek help from people or groups who can facilitate the art of talking to each other.

All over the country there are family therapists specializing in communication difficulties in remarriages and stepfamilies. Check with friends who might have had similar problems for recommendations.

The American Group Psychotherapy Association is a national organization headquartered in New York City with 27 local chapters. It will refer you to therapists in your area specializing in remarital issues.

The Academy of Family Mediators based in Eugene, Oregon, will send you a list of mediators in your area trained to help resolve all family disputes, whether they're support, custody, asset distribution, or parent/child conflicts. Mediation, because it forces you to talk to each other and resolve your own differences, has become a powerful tool in resolving family monetary problems.

The Stepfamily Association of America, headquartered in Lincoln, Nebraska, with local chapters in every major U.S. city, is a national self-help group. Its supportive camaraderie and vast materials are valuable in helping remarrieds deal and heal. Laughter, tears, and a slew of good coping suggestions pepper the monthly meetings. Opening up to others helps you open up to each other. Listening to others helps you learn to listen to each other. The organization was founded in 1979 by two mental health professionals, John Visher, a psychiatrist, and Emily Visher, a psychologist, themselves remarried and very befuddled at first by how to handle their new family.

"I heard about the SAA about four years after we were married, and we went to a few meetings," relays Peter, a systems analyst on Long Island. "I guess we were having some problems with my kids — even though they weren't living with us. The topic for one of the meetings was vacations and, boy, was I ready for this. It seemed to me we never saw each other anymore. Libby and I were both working long hours. We had just bought a house which was a wreck. When we weren't trying to fix it up, we were with my kids. I was drained of all energy — psychic and physical. I don't know what prompted me to open up and share these feelings with the group, but I did. I even told them I wanted to go to Mexico on a vacation. Libby hadn't known of that before this particular evening. She turned white, as if she was undergoing a spinal tap.

"We talked all the way home and long into the next morning."

"I had never realized the depth of Peter's need to go away before he mentioned it at the meeting," Libby says. "And I didn't really understand why I was so opposed to it. It was kind of a reflex reaction to growing up poor — we can't afford it, we can't take the time off now, that sort of thing. Our talking forced me to look at the reality of the situation, which was that I had just gotten a 20% raise [following a move into management in city government] and that I, too, was exhausted. Surely we deserved this trip. We hadn't even taken a weekend to ourselves since our honeymoon.

"Still, I couldn't get myself to make the reservations. Peter had to do that. And to assure myself that I was worthy of the trip, I worked myself into a state of exhaustion the week before, staying at the office every night until 11. I fell asleep on the way to the airport, woke up long enough to walk onto the plane, and then slept again for five hours. When we finally landed in Puerto Vallarta, I looked around and couldn't thank Peter enough." Says Libby, "I'll always be grateful for that meeting which forced Peter to talk and me to listen."

Comfort quotients differ when it comes to sharing thoughts, information, and feelings. But for a couple to get through the better or worse, richer or poorer times, so that they get better and richer, honest, regular communication is essential.

Chapter 3

Prenuptial Agreements
Terms of Endearment?

DID YOU KNOW . . .
- The divorce rate is higher for second marriages than for first marriages.
- Of second-marriage divorces, 40% will occur within the first four years of the wedding.
- Couples in which one or both of the partners have been married before are more likely to have a prenuptial agreement than people marrying for the first time.

Real people don't have prenuptial agreements. Or at least not most of the real middle- and upper-middle-class people I interviewed. Even if they were prime candidates for prenups — and there are many such people — many shied away from them. Interestingly, lawyers and financial planners, those very people who urge everyone with any assets whatsoever to "put something in writing" (why not? the little "something" nets a nice fee), don't always heed their own advice. Randi and Roger Smith are a remarried Florida couple whose personal and business lives meshed five years ago when they became Smith & Smith, financial planners. Their rationale for not having an agreement, according to Roger: "We didn't need it. She came into the marriage with cash. I came in with the business. I accepted both the financial and time liability of her children."

"I don't tell people they should *have* one," says a Tucson financial planner, "just that they should *consider* it. We didn't have one. We have fairly equal assets and almost the same number of children. He has four. I have five."

So, what does this mean? Should or shouldn't we be concerned about spelling out in advance of the remarriage how property we own is to be split in the event of divorce or death? Are we as concerned about divorce (and its perilous negotiations leading to a division of property) as we should be? Or is there too much emphasis on the subject of pre-nuptial agreements (also called antenuptial agreements) and too much pressure from financial advisers and friends to have them?

Why People Don't Have Them

For most people the subject is moot — there's not enough in the way of assets to discuss. "That's something rich people can worry about, not us" is the typical response when a prenuptial is mentioned.

Others, still in the blush of romance, believe in each other. Rightly or wrongly, they figure that the union will survive until death (when all that's needed is a will) or, if in the unlikely event they do divorce, that they will be able to work out an amicable way to divide property.

Some feel they are already protected. And they may be right. Most state laws provide spouses with limited financial protection, so in the majority of cases, they won't wind up penniless in case of death or divorce.

And then there are people who might want to draw up a contract but who are afraid to bring up the subject. They feel it's unromantic to plan a divorce at the same time they're planning a wedding. Or they don't want to cast themselves in an unfavorable light for fear "she'll think I don't trust her" or "he'll think I want to marry him only for his money."

Prenuptials Are Explosive

"I've never been part of a prenuptial that didn't generate some resentment," says one New York attorney, who claims to have drafted over 150. "Even those done for all the right reasons and which are eminently fair by my standards."

Why?

There's an inherent paradox in a prenuptial. Says Mark Levinson, a Boston attorney: "By reducing a relationship to an agreement, you drain it. There's a realization that no agreement is worth the paper it's written on, if someone decides to break it. All you have to do is look at the Trumps' well-publicized debacle."

Or perhaps by concentrating on financial matters surrounding death and divorce you lose sight of a larger picture of love and commitment.

In cases where one is adamant about an agreement and the other less so, the process of drafting one sets resentment in motion. The tacit or voiced feeling: "If you loved me, you'd want me to have everything of yours or, at the very least, access to everything — even though I don't want to touch it."

"Even when the person in the weaker financial picture tries to disavow his or her interest in the whole process," Levinson says of the scenario where one is pressing for the agreement, "as we go through it, tension builds."

"I represented the husband in an agreement he had never wanted," says a New Mexico attorney. "He was a teacher; she was well-to-do — family money, high-paying job. After they were married, he became fanatic about keeping everything separate. He admitted that the reason was that he was angry with her for initiating the prenuptial. He wanted her to live with the fact that what was hers was hers and what was his was his."

Perhaps the most significant reason given by financial and psychological advisers who oppose prenuptials is that they're unrealistic. They give disproportionate significance to financial issues; then they try to solve these issues in a telescoped period of time — the time it takes to draw up, negotiate, and sign an agreement. Permanent financial resolutions can't be rushed by the deadline of a wedding date, and temporary issues can change or evolve, they argue.

Prenuptials are temporary — or at least should be. Since it's impossible to anticipate events far in advance of their happening, prenuptials become outdated (though not necessarily invalid) quickly. "For months prior to our wedding we argued about a provision dealing with a sizable piece of property my husband owned," a Houston entrepreneur says. "Two years later that property had to be sold to pay off debts on his failing business. All the negotiating Ken and I did was for naught. What we were left with was enormous ill will that now has to be mended."

So the question is, Is a prenuptial agreement a self-fulfilling prophecy leading to divorce or a breakup even before the marriage?

Some experts insist it is not — that the process of drawing up a prenuptial is prophylactic. "If the premarital discussion of money ends in no marriage at all, I don't think of it as having obstructed a marriage," says New York matrimonial attorney Jacalyn F. Barnett. "I think of it as having prevented a divorce."

Others question its value and postulate that there is a higher incidence of divorce among those with prenuptials than among those without them because the people who want them reveal a lack of commitment at the onset of the remarriage. Even if this were true, there might be other reasons for a future divorce among people signing prenuptial agreements. Resentment stemming from a feeling of being maneuvered into signing a prenuptial might be one. Another might be that people who draw up prenuptials generally have more money than those who don't and can more easily *afford* to divorce.

It's the Process That Counts

Even if a prenuptial pact is not for everyone, the prenuptial *process* is. Talking about finances before the wedding widens the middle ground of trust that a couple needs for a successful marriage.

What should you be talking about — prenuptially?

The financial facts. What is each of you bringing to the marriage in the way of property (everything from assets to stock holdings), debts (from alimony and support payments to credit card balances), obligations (from support for parents to pledges to charities), and expected income (from every source)? Add to that the other bits and pieces of financial information that complete the picture, such as how much life insurance you have and who the beneficiaries are, where you bank, what's in your safe deposit box, and how much retirement savings you have. Even if you don't plan to have a prenuptial agreement, you should draw up a list of what you're each bringing into the marriage in the way of assets. Then date it and sign it. In the event of a divorce, this paper can be used to trace the ownership of assets.

The financial considerations you will be facing immediately. Chances are you've had enough time together to know what they are. Do your spending styles clash? Are you going to have to move to a bigger home or apartment because of the additional children who will be either living with you or coming to visit? Do you expect additional financial pressure from your former spouse? Is there going to be a significant decrease in household income when one of you loses your monthly alimony? These issues have to be addressed — and solutions sought.

What each of you would be entitled to by state law in case of divorce or death without a prenuptial agreement. Nobody wants to think about these when entering a remarriage. But the possibilities for either exist and you need to play out the worst-case scenarios:

1. You're getting a divorce and you have to go to court and let a judge decide the terms of a separation agreement because you and your spouse can't negotiate one yourselves. (That's the least desirable alternative because of its emotional and financial toll, and because it rarely offers creative solutions that would meet your particular needs.) In most equitable distribution states, if the courts have to decide who gets what in a divorce it will ask you both to put all your assets on the proverbial table. Then anything that either of you owned prior to marriage is removed. Next to go is anything that either of you received during the time of the marriage as a gift, inheritance, or bequest under a will. What's left is usually split. Community property states — Arizona, California, Louisiana, Idaho, Nevada, New Mexico, Texas, Washington, and Wisconsin — are the toughest in enforcing the equal division of assets in case of divorce.

2. One of you dies. Most state laws protect a spouse from being totally disinherited. States vary as to the minimum share of the deceased spouse's property a surviving spouse is entitled to — but generally it's one third. In a few states, it's a half.

Because state laws vary widely, it's important to ask an attorney what the divorce and inheritance laws are in your state and talk about what sort of an impact they might have on you.

Drawing up a will. Being skittish about discussing death when you're beginning a new life is understandable. But not smart. Having a will is even more important in a subsequent marriage than a first marriage because your estate is so much more complex and because your wishes may be counter to how the state would dispose of your property if you died without a will (intestate). (Estate planning is discussed more fully in Chapter 10.)

The subject of "fairness." One of the biggest thorns in a remarriage is the fact that the financial seesaw is not level. One of you is usually the financial "heavy" and the other the "lightweight." That imbalance may not ever be shifted.

There may be one person who's "giving up" an important asset for the remarriage. Consider Marjorie, a New York City woman who lives in a large, rent-controlled apartment. She is marrying Donald and moving into his home. What would happen if the marriage doesn't work out and they were to divorce? She'd have to move out and her housing costs would be many times what she had previously paid in rent. What's fair? Perhaps in recognition of her giving up her rent-controlled apartment, Marjorie should be made a joint owner of Donald's home. Perhaps a prenuptial agreement should provide for a substantial alimony payment if they divorce, one that would pay for an apartment comparable to the one Marjorie vacated.

The fairness issue creeps in before the wedding, in the early years of the remarriage, and even years later. "Her children get more money from their grandparents each year than I'd be able to give my children in a lifetime." "If I have to put up with his crass family all the time, why shouldn't I be entitled to half his inheritance?" "What's a fair amount to spend on entertaining my children, who visit once a month, as opposed to her daughter, who lives with us?" "Our baby is entitled to more than his two teenagers."

A couple has to define fairness when it comes to the extended family. Is it equality? Is it each according to need? Is it yours is yours, mine is mine? Is it determined on an incident-by-incident basis?

Your goals and how you'll finance them. You've probably shared dreams; they may even be part of the bond you have with one another. They could include having children, buying a second home by the seashore, starting your own business, changing careers, retiring on a forty-acre farm. Whatever they are, they need a plan to finance them.

Prime Candidates for Prenuptials

I attended a wedding recently where both he and she were remarrying; he for the fourth time, she for the third. The minister was asking them to repeat some very traditional vows, I thought. The last one they exchanged was "With all my worldly goods, I thee endow." On both sides of the aisle, the bride's and the groom's, there was an audible gulp and then some whispering. All the invited guests knew of the financial trials and tribulations at least one of the partners had gone through during a previous divorce. But we weren't sure the minister had the same information. And we all wondered, some silently and some more brazenly later, if they were indeed joining all their financial forces.

There are some remarrying people for whom the prenuptial contract works:

• *Couples remarrying later in life* — when they've built up a sizable estate and there are adult children.

• *Couples in which one spouse is giving up something substantial in order to enter this marriage.* A woman who gives up her career to bring up his children. A man who postpones retirement so that he will be in a better position to help support his new wife and her children.

• *Couples who both want it.* They are usually composed of two extremely independent, financially successful people. Sometimes they feel they had to give up too much in a prior divorce and therefore are very protective about assets. Sometimes they want to guard their financial autonomy because they have invested so much of themselves in developing it.

• *Couples in which one spouse (or both) is an entrepreneur.* Nobody benefits when the long-term success of a business is threatened by divorce or death. So the entrepreneur might want to separate it from other marital property and make independent provisions for the business's succession and survival.

• *Couples in which one spouse doesn't have complete faith in the other.* This is not to say that trust won't develop — in time. It's just that it's not there now. (Under the best of circumstances, these people shouldn't marry until they feel more comfortable with one another. But that's not always the reality.)

What Makes a Fair Agreement?

• *An agreement that protects and comforts both of you.* For the contract to be a stepping-stone to a committed relationship, it also has to be created in a spirit that's caring and protective of the two partners.

• *Full and fair disclosure of what each of your individual assets and financial liabilities are.* That's hard for some people. Says one matrimonial attorney: "I have found that one of the most pervasive secrets men have is how much support and alimony they have to pay. When male clients come in to discuss a prenuptial agreement and I tell them they have to reveal their alimony and support obligations, about 10% walk out and never return. The issue of how much they pay seems to be an embarrassment." The attorney, a woman, says that women, on the other hand, generally want their future spouses to know how considerable their support from a former husband is, "so that the new husband can appreciate how much alimony they're giving up for this union."

• *You have to enter into the agreement voluntarily.* If, at any time, you feel your new mate is holding your feet to the fire because of mortification, financial devastation, or betrayal he or she experienced in a prior relationship ("I want this because I want to make sure you don't do to me what Betty did"), or you're feeling coerced into making concessions ("I'll call the wedding off unless you sign"), back away and review the situation. You shouldn't be punished in advance for someone else's sins. Nor should you be threatened into signing. In line with that, the agreement should be signed by both of you as far in advance of the wedding date as possible (at least one month) or else it feels like a shakedown (and might be interpreted as such if challenged later on).

• *You have to understand the provisions in the agreement and their potential ramifications to you.* For your own safety and to make certain the agreement holds up in the event of a later challenge, both of you need separate legal representation. No matter how comfortable you feel with the attorney who's drawing up the agreement, hire another lawyer to review it to protect your interests. If one of you is wealthy and the other would find it an economic hardship to retain a lawyer, the richer person should offer to pay for the other's counsel, but in *no way* should the payer have any say in the choice of the independent counsel selected by his or her fiancé.

What to Think About Before Seeing an Attorney

Since the purpose of a prenuptial agreement is to spell out how to split the property you hold individually and jointly in case of a divorce or death, you should think about how you'd handle the following . . . and the consequences of your actions:

• *Property you each brought to the marriage.* In most cases, you'll want to retain sole ownership of these properties. In cases where one person owns everything going into the marriage, he or she may want to consider transferring some assets to the other person a bit at a time. If real property is transferred, it must be conveyed in a legal fashion, including recording the transaction with governmental authorities, and should be done after the marriage to avoid taxes.

In some states if one or both of you is bringing property into this marriage that you intend to keep as yours (such as a country home or shares of stock) and want to make certain the income from these assets remains yours as well, all you have to do is sign a unilateral statement that says the income from this individual property shall henceforth be individual and not marital. That statement must be notarized and given to your spouse within a certain number of days of its signing. The nice thing about this is that if that's all you're concerned about, you don't need a full-blown prenuptial agreement.

• *Property obtained during the marriage.* In most states, property obtained during the marriage will be considered jointly owned when it's divided during a divorce, unless proven to be otherwise.

• *The increase in value during the time of the marriage of property you own separately.* Suppose the property is improved or taxes or upkeep are paid out of money in a joint account, how should the increase in value be assessed? What happens if, when they enter the marriage, each spouse had 100 shares of a different blue-chip stock. They divorce four years later. One's stock has quadrupled in value and the other's is worthless because the company went bankrupt.

• *Pension and employee benefits and insurance.* Who are the beneficiaries? Are they determined by a separation agreement from a prior marriage? Will the new spouse be sufficiently protected in case of death?

• *Preexisting debts and liabilities.* When a person has debts to repay, it means that, by definition, less goes into the marital pool. Should there be recognition of the fact that one partner is using marital assets to pay off premarital debts? Should the other spouse be compensated for this?

• *Compensation for someone who is making a financial sacrifice.* Will there be a transfer of home ownership into joint names, for example, if the woman suspends her career to stay home to care for his children?

• *Support for children from previous marriages.* Will he pay for her children's Ivy League college tuitions the same way he pays them for his children? Will she dip into her savings for his daughter's therapy?

• *Support and division of property in case of divorce.* This is the fail-safe provision — the negotiation of a separation agreement prior to the actual event. In the case of support, there are generally three ways of handling it: complete waiver of support rights; a lump-sum payment; or periodic payments.

• *How the terms for rights to your estate or property might vary depending on factors such as the length of the marriage or the birth of children.* For example, a couple might agree that the wife is entitled to 5% of her husband's premarital assets for each year of marriage — to a maximum of 50%. So in 5 years, she'd be entitled to 25%; in 10 years, 50%.

Forget about including any mention of who's going to care for the children, do the housework, take the cat to the vet's, the religion in which you're going to raise the children, or any other life-style matters. Most courts won't enforce these clauses, though the inclusion of these clauses rarely invalidates the prenuptial agreement's other provisions.

The courts are especially protective of children. Their support and well-being cannot be threatened by either parent's signing a prenuptial agreement. Nor can you preordain what's to happen to them. "I refused to do a prenuptial agreement involving a man marrying a woman with a child from a former marriage because he wanted a provision which said if they had a child and the marriage dissolved, he would get this child — since she already had one," says one New York attorney. "If they had two children, he wanted his choice of child. And if there were three, he'd select two of them. Basically, he wanted the pick of the litter. As I heard later, they didn't get married."

Who Should Draw It Up

You can draw up a simple agreement that says, basically, "Here's what each of us owns today, and it'll be mine if the marriage dissolves. Anything we acquire during marriage will be split 50-50." Attach the document to a schedule of possessions, have it notarized, and you have an executed prenuptial agreement that most courts will uphold. For an added measure of safety, ask a lawyer to review it and give an opinion as to whether or not it will stand up in court. But don't be talked into an extensive document — unless, of course, you feel you need it.

Use a matrimonial lawyer if you are not a do-it-yourselfer or if your assets are entangled, complex, or numerous. Most are experienced at drawing up prenuptials and adept at running their clients through the prenuptial "what-ifs."

"It's interesting that even though people may have decided to go ahead with a prenuptial, they come to my office not wanting to bring up their private agendas," Boston attorney Mark Levinson says. "They look to me to speak the unspeakable. So I do. I say, 'Let's take some absurd scenarios. You get married Friday night and on Saturday one of you takes off. How would you want your finances divided then?' From there it becomes easier to discuss other scenarios."

Depending on the complexity of the agreement and the address of the law firm that designs it (Park Avenue firms in New York have greater overhead than Main Street firms in Tennessee), legal fees for the drafting attorney will run from $500 to several thousand dollars. Be certain to have a complete understanding in advance of what the fee arrangements will be. Most lawyers will require a retainer, an up-front payment. Insist on a letter of agreement from the attorney outlining the amount of the retainer and the scope of what it covers, the hourly rate of each attorney who will work on the matter, a statement that the retainer represents an advance against the time actually spent on the matter, and definition as to who will be responsible for expenses and what the lawyer means by expenses (you may be asked to pick up photocopying charges or the attorney's lunch bills if he works through lunch).

Scale down the number of hours your attorney will have to put into this project by doing some preliminary work, arranging your financial records, having a financial statement ready, and outlining who's related to whom (see the "About the Family" and "What We Own" worksheets outlined in Chapter 10).

And remember: Each of you must be represented by your own attorney.

When, Why, and How to Amend or Negate a Prenuptial

As a marriage matures and as life changes, so must a prenuptial agreement. It's necessary to initiate periodic updates based on

- events (you have a child together, one of you gets seriously ill, you have financial responsibility for your spouse's parent)
- the number of years married (you have a very different relationship ten years into the remarriage than you had when you signed the agreement)
- a shift in tax, estate, or marital laws

Whether an agreement is amended or negated, it can't be done unilaterally. Both of you must agree in writing to changes. And both of you should sign the additions or a statement of dissolution before a notary public.

You can negate an agreement three ways. Destroy the original and all the copies of it. Or draw an x through it (and all copies), write "No longer valid," and initial and date every page. Or draw up a statement that says you both have agreed to negate the agreement, then sign it in front of a notary public.

Anatomy of a Prenuptial — In Stages

For Tandy and Robert the prenuptial agreement they signed just two weeks before their marriage was really the *third* version of a pact they had drafted two years previously when they began to live together and, without lawyers, negotiated a cohabitation agreement. You would think that after this agreement and another agreement drawn up when they were engaged, the prenuptial would have been a snap. It wasn't. "Those final negotiations were wrenching," says Robert. His ambivalence about the process is evident when he says, "No one can convince me it's like a partnership agreement. In business you provide for the success of a partnership in addition to what happens in a split-up. But the sole purpose of a prenuptial is what to do in case of a dissolution. There is nothing positive in that. Yet I probably would go through it again. The agreement was important to both of us."

The facts: Tandy is in her late 30s, divorced, with custody of one daughter, aged nine. A couple of years prior to her divorce five years ago, she founded a service business in Detroit. The business has done nicely, not sensationally; but it is on the verge of franchising.

Robert is in his mid-40s and has two children — one a freshman in college, the other a freshman in high school. He was divorced six years ago. Recently Robert sold an eminently successful business and realized an enormous profit. By his own estimation he is "very sound financially . . . and cash flush."

Agreement #1. "I didn't realize what an emotional and financial commitment it was going to be when we moved in together," Tandy says. "First, I rented out my small house and he bought a large one — big enough for us, my daughter, and his visiting teenagers. That meant if we broke up, I'd have to find another place to live. I couldn't kick the renters out — and my daughter would have to change school districts. I started to have flashbacks of what happened in my first marriage where I got creamed financially — and emotionally. I felt a cohabitation agreement would help me deal with the anxiety. I needed to have in writing that in case we wanted to separate, Robert would come to at least two months of therapy with me so that I could fully understand the reasons behind the split. My former husband didn't. He was here one day, gone the next — to another woman. And because I didn't want to experience the same frightening feeling of being penniless that I had before, I wanted Robert to assure me of some money to rent a place in the same school district and to see my daughter and me through any therapy we needed."

"Although I didn't mind the discussion, I was offended by a cohabitation agreement," Robert says. "I felt 'We have this wonderful life together, why would you want to screw it up with a signed document?' I knew I would help Tandy financially if we were to break up."

The discussions were bruising — so much so that they sought the help of a family therapist, then a psychologist. They dug for the underlying reasons for their attitudes.

"Robert is a wonderful, open man, ready to listen to my concerns, even though he might not understand or agree with them," Tandy says.

"I wasn't used to discussing financial issues with my mate — I've always made the decisions — and had to learn the process," Robert says.

Agreement #2. At about the time an engagement ring was slipped onto Tandy's finger, the couple decided to draw up a second agreement. It was constructed as an add-on to the cohabitation agreement. Whoever left the house would have to sell his or her share to the other person (as if Tandy were joint owner). Since Tandy didn't have the money she would need to do that if Robert left, Robert established an account for Tandy for just that purpose. Robert also took out an insurance policy naming Tandy as beneficiary. They drew up new wills, naming each other as executors but still leaving their respective estates to their children. Again, the contract was self-drawn and self-executed.

Agreement #3. The prenuptial. "We thought we could do this ourselves, too," Robert says. "We couldn't. First of all, we didn't know what the state laws were and if we were violating them. For example, we had a sexual fidelity clause in it initially where we agreed to give up 50% of any marital property if we violated that clause. This, the lawyers told us, was too punitive and wouldn't stand up in court. Also, we were dealing with more . . . and more complex . . . issues. The inequality of what we're bringing into the marriage, for one. And that's always been a source of conflict. We went as far as we could go in our own negotiations and then said, 'Let your attorney talk to mine.' "

Tandy: "Robert's financial success in business is shielded from me because it came before we were married. But mine will probably happen during our marriage. Does that mean I should share equally everything I've struggled to build simply because he married me at a better time? That wouldn't be fair. So we've made some compromises. The growth in my business will not be considered marital property; the appreciation on a piece of property he owns won't either.

"If our reasons for having a prenuptial weren't so valid," Tandy says, two months after the wedding, "I don't think we would have survived the process. But the agreement will last because it was drawn up in a spirit of fairness, love, and respect and built on a foundation of openness and trust. It has helped us solidify our emotional commitment and delineate the balance of power. And we've *almost* learned how to resolve conflict."

One More Building Block

Whether or not you have a prenuptial agreement, you must flush out your immediate financial concerns (which are almost always entwined with emotional ones). For most people, the prenuptial *process* will be enough, especially if you maintain mutual respect and a sense of fairness during the discussions.

If, indeed, you are candidates for a prenuptial agreement, tackle the process logically. First, understand the emotional reasons behind your position and your prospective spouse's. Second, go about the business of drawing up a prenuptial in a businesslike manner. Third, come up with a document that both of you consider fair. If you are looking for a committed relationship, consider the prenuptial as terms of endearment.

Success builds on itself. The better you can address today's problems, the more triumphant you will be in meeting the other financial issues faced over the course of the marriage.

Chapter 4

Your Home
Moving In, Moving Out, Moving On

DID YOU KNOW . . .
- Divorced parents move around: 12% live in a different state one year after divorce or separation. That percentage increases to 25 after three years and to 40 after eight years.
- Having children (step or biological) in the house, being relatively young, and being well educated are positive factors associated with a remarried family's integration into a community and involvement in community life.

Often the first order of financial business a remarried couple must address is where to live.

Home for remarrieds is not only where they hang their proverbial hats.

It may be where your wife's former husband also hung his.

It may be where your husband's first wife conceived their children, petted their dog, and cooked their dinner.

It may be your new spouse's bachelor apartment or the place you've been raising your children as a single parent.

It may be new space to both of you.

None of those might be to your liking. You may feel like

an intruder, a person living with someone else's history, a stranger in an uncomfortable house, or a transplant.

Merging households means that as a couple you'll save money. But it is always difficult, whether it's done someplace new or in a place where one of you has been living. Yet there's an air of excitement, of adventure about it. There is no universally "right" place to live when you remarry. Whether you're moving in or moving out, it's important to move on and develop your own identity as a couple in a home that reflects the two of you.

A Home of Your Own

"I'll never feel comfortable in this house," Marty says. "This house" is a Colonial that Darlene bought when she was married to her first husband, a house in which she and her son had lived for four and a half years before Marty moved in. "Even if Darlene consults with me on changes, I feel it's hers. I don't feel entitled to make decisions. Something as simple as which wallpaper we hang in the bathroom doesn't seem like my domain. I prune the hedges with trepidation. I'd trim them down just fractionally because I hesitate to take liberties with her property. I can't wait until we can afford to sell this house and buy one that's ours."

Most couples want to write the first chapter of their new marriage in a home neither has lived in before. If you can afford it and there are no mitigating factors, such as the need for you or a family member to be near a special school, doctor, or instructor, or a separation agreement that prohibits the move until a child is of a certain age, then, from a psychological standpoint, neutral space is a good way to start life together.

Not that it's easy. Husband, wife, and all the children living with you will feel a little shaky on this new foundation. That can be positive. You're sharing an emotion and an experience: anxiety in your new surroundings.

"I didn't anticipate that the move across town would be a big deal," says Jane, a human resources manager for a large New York company. *"But it was. My daughter had to change elementary schools, which meant she had to establish new friendships. She was bitter about that. My husband, Chuck, found the commute into the city longer and more annoying than when he lived in a condo right off the highway. And I hated the neighbors. One had a tea to introduce me to the women on the street soon after we moved in. It was awful. I was put on review. They were brazen with their questions. 'Had I lived with Chuck before we bought this house?' 'Was he the reason for my divorce or was I the reason for his?' 'Did we plan on having children of our own?' I remember coming home afterwards and crying bitterly, certain we had made a mistake moving away from areas that we knew.*

"It has worked out," reports Jane, three years after the move. *"When she went to middle school, my daughter felt like a queen bee. She knew just about everyone — the kids from her old elementary school and those from her new one. Chuck has adapted to the longer car ride and likes having a house to putter in. And I've become friendly — not friends — with these suburban homemakers who never before had known a remarried woman."*

Make no mistake about it, however, a home of your own is not necessarily a panacea. Ellen, an Atlanta psychotherapist, didn't find the new house curative. "Before I was remarried, I owned a home bought with the $10,000 inheritance I received from my parents. It was just big enough for me and my two girls. I was proud of it. It was my symbolic and real financial security. When I remarried, I sold it and used the profits for a down payment on the large home Dale and I jointly owned. Years later, I realized that I had resented doing this. The first reason was the $10,000 — which had grown to $25,000 by the time I sold the small house — represented something like a birthright to me, especially since I'd grown up in a poor family. I didn't want to share it. And second was that, even though Dale was paying for the upkeep, this new house was much more costly to maintain. I worried that if Dale and I were to split up, I wouldn't be able to afford it. I felt at risk. What I didn't realize then, but do now, was that my investment in the small house represented my personal struggle for identity."

Ellen and Dale's unique resolution: Dale returned Ellen's down payment to her. With that money, she bought a condominium that she does with as she pleases. At different times she has rented it out or allowed her two college-aged daughters to live there rent-free. Once, during an eight-month separation from Dale, she lived there. Dale owns the house. They have informally agreed that should they separate the house will be his — though he has willed it to Ellen should he die before she does.

Selling Your Old Place

Most people can't afford to buy another house before their first one is sold (or, at least, don't feel financially comfortable with the idea). So, in the case of a remarriage, it might mean waiting until both of you go to contract on your respective homes before you seriously make offers for one of your own (although you should have been looking all the while). In tight real estate markets, waiting could take a year or more. Then, there's another consideration. One or both of you might own a home with a former spouse who, according to a separation or divorce agreement, has to be consulted on and agree to any sale of that property. If the spouse resents the new marriage or wants to nettle you, he or she might arbitrarily claim the price being offered is too low and try to thwart the sale. In that case, you'll have to follow the procedures to settle the dispute outlined in your separation agreement.

If you want to sell quickly, you must be willing to sell at a fair price. A reasonable price (determined by appraisals from three or four brokers in the area plus checking the recent selling prices of comparable area homes) will draw more buyers than a high one tagged "negotiable." And dropping the price of the house below a benchmark figure like $200,000 often helps.

Consider an auction if selling quickly is important. About 5% of all houses now are sold through auctions — a sales technique that is used more frequently when the economy, and especially the real estate market, falters. The best way not to take a beating at auction is to set a minimum reserve price on your home. If bidders don't meet or exceed it, there's no sale.

What if, in a rush of enthusiasm, you buy a house together before either or both of you has sold the old house because you didn't need the cash from the sale of one to buy another?

In slow markets, when sellers squirm and buyers become ferocious bargainers, you might consider renting for a while. It means you'll have to postpone selling — which could be a blessing if the real estate market shows signs of coming to life soon. If you rent the house furnished, it provides you with storage opportunities for some of the duplicate pieces of furniture you probably are bringing to this marriage. And renting a furnished home or condo on a short-term basis is attractive to many people who are just moving to a locale.

The best renter is a prospective buyer who will lease your home with an option to buy. This arrangement allows the lessee to apply some portion of the rent toward a purchase, say at the end of a year. It can be structured in such a way as to make the future purchase more appealing, such as by assigning 50% of the monthly rent toward the down payment. The renter then has to contemplate how much money is lost if he or she walks away without buying at the end of the rental period.

Keep in mind the tax rules. You don't have to live in the house to take advantage of the tax deferment given those who sell a principal residence and acquire another at the same or a higher price within two years. But you have to prove to the IRS that you're renting as a stopgap measure, that the rental was meant to be brief. And during the time of the rental you can still deduct mortgage interest and property tax — though, of course, you must claim the rent as income. (For people 55 or over, there are important additional tax consequences related to selling; refer to Chapter 9, "Remarrying after the Children Are Grown.")

Buying a Home Together

Whether an apartment in the gate house of an estate or the estate itself, a home represents a haven. Even more than what we wear, it reflects our personalities, our interests, our attitudes, our needs, our tastes, *and* the state of our finances.

Normal differences must be resolved when two people decide to buy a home together, such as whether you want to climb stairs, live in a socioeconomically homogeneous neighborhood, feel uncomfortable if your neighbor's kitchen window is 10 feet from yours, prefer a Tudor or split-level. A remarried couple has additional considerations.

1. Where will you buy? In a community where the children living with you are going to school? Close to noncustodial children so you can see them frequently? Near supportive relatives or friends? In a community where one of you lived before? Far from a former spouse?

2. Who is responsible for the down payment and the mortgage? This becomes a particularly thorny problem when one of the spouses has considerably more money than the other — a situation more common in remarriages than in first marriages.

3. What's the best way for the house to be titled, taking into consideration estate plans and the possibility of divorce?

4. Are you planning to have children of your own? If the answer is "yes," should you buy a place you can grow into?

5. Can you afford and do you want to provide bedrooms for children who visit? Whether you have a "child-in-every-bedroom" home or not, you'll want to provide visiting children with comfortable space of their own (no matter how small), so they don't feel like intruders when they sleep over.

Who Owns the House . . . Emotionally?

Larry and Miriam are engaged. But the question of home ownership has become such a thorn that unless they can resolve it, they probably will not get married. Larry, a New York City architect who hasn't been married before, has a net worth of $350,000. That's about 50 times that of his fiancée's. "I never thought of the difference in our assets or our earnings until we began to talk about buying a house. Miriam, a social worker who has been supporting her two children, each from a different marriage, couldn't contribute to the down payment on a $275,000 house. I knew that. But I didn't think she would expect equal ownership. She does," Larry says.

"I have mixed feelings about that," he admits.

Legally, in most equitable distribution states, property *might* be considered separate during a divorce action if one spouse buys the house before marriage from money he or she had before the marriage, never transfers the title to joint ownership, and maintains the house as a separate property during the marriage by paying for everything connected with the house — mortgage, utilities, repairs, or additions — for the entire time the couple lives in the house. At that time, if they couldn't negotiate a settlement, a court would usually balance Larry's separate ownership with what it considers fair in these circumstances. It might take into consideration Larry's intent when he purchased the house, why he wanted separate ownership, Miriam's expectations, how long they lived there together as husband and wife, their needs, and their other assets. In community property states, "fair" isn't considered. In those states, virtually all assets that a couple owns or *develops* together during a marriage are automatically deemed the property of both. So if Larry and Miriam lived in a community property state and if Miriam were to pay the mortgage a few times or pay for a new roof, the courts would probably say she had a half interest in the house because she had been part of its development.

The only way to ensure that the house remains separate is to draw up a pre- or postnuptial agreement that both parties willingly sign.

Is "separate" the best way to own a home, though?

Not necessarily.

Mention "home" and people think of roots, security, permanence, commitment, financial security, and stability. All compelling feelings for married couples. That's why "home ownership" figures so prominently in the minds of people — especially people who have been hurt or disappointed in a prior marriage. So when one spouse "owns" the home, it's as if he or she has a lock on roots, security, and permanence, while the other spouse is shut out of them. It's psychologically unequal. The non-owning spouse might justly wonder "Why even bother buying a new place to live? Why not just move into your present abode? It would make me feel just as uneasy, insecure, and financially at sea as living in a new house that I don't have an ownership interest in."

Larry's resistance to buying the house jointly reflects a tentative commitment to the relationship. He wants roots and security, he says, "but never having shared a life with anyone before, I'm plenty scared. I keep thinking that when I sign a check for $55,000 for the down payment, it's like I'm giving Miriam a $27,500 gift — even before we're married. And then, though I don't expect her to contribute much to the upkeep of the house, if we were to separate she'd get half of it. That doesn't seem fair to me."

Miriam admits her desire for ownership is also rooted in skittishness about the marriage. "My track record for marriages isn't great," she says. "I've made two mistakes — bad ones. While I don't think Larry is anything like my other two husbands, I'm unsure and trying to protect myself and my children — at least financially."

If their relationship lasts long enough to make it to the altar, Miriam and Larry are going to have to play to the strengths of a marriage. Commitment and trust have to be introduced.

One workable solution would be for Miriam to contribute toward the down payment. A real stake in this house would serve to minimize Larry's control and his resentment. Even $2,000 (of her $7,000 savings) to Larry's $53,000 would go a long way. It says, "I'm willing to take a financial risk on this because I love you and trust in our future." For Larry to understand the depth of the commitment he'd have to do some math. Miriam's $2,000 represents about 30% of her savings; his $53,000 is 15% of his.

Taking Title: In Whose Name Should the Property Be?

As we have just said, title is less important in divorce than in death. Many states assume that a married couple's contribution to a home they live in is equal, no matter whose name is on the deed. Thus, in a divorce, the property is usually split equally, unless some other division seems more fair or equitable or an agreement can be reached by the spouses outside the court's domain.

For remarried couples, *how* the house is owned is far more pressing at the time of one of their deaths — especially if one or both of the spouses want to leave some or all of their share of the home to a child from a former marriage.

Usually a couple buys a home jointly as *joint tenants* with what's called a right of survivorship. That means when one dies, the other automatically becomes the sole owner. Holding title this way is best for remarrying couples with no or young children. It also works well for couples who want their spouses to have sole ownership when one dies, so that the survivor can continue living in the home without interference or sell it and use the profits to maintain a life-style.

Holding a home as joint tenants means that one spouse can insist upon the sale of that property at any time even if the other one resists. It also permits the cash value of the property to be used to satisfy debt obligation incurred by either of the spouses.

Couples who want to leave their ownership share in the house to children from a former marriage should consider ownership as *tenants in common*. Then, in your will you declare to whom you want to leave your share of the house. There are complications, though. Dividing a bank account after a death is a lot simpler than dividing a house.

Spouses can own homes separately, *as individuals*. Sole owners can sell the house, mortgage it, or will it without the consent of a spouse. They're in full control of the property. What they often find during times of divorce, however, is that unless the separate ownership was clearly spelled out in a prenuptial agreement, property they thought was separate is marital. Where one of the partners owns the home and has grown children who he or she eventually wants to inherit the house, many people establish a marital life estate trust. It's a way of assuring the surviving spouse of the use and comfort of the home for as long as he or she lives. The children are entitled to the property only after the surviving spouse's death. (For more estate planning information, see Chapter 10.)

Moving In

Marty and Darlene's desire for a place of their own was put on hold for a number of reasons. He had just taken a new job and didn't feel secure enough in it to risk a move that was certain to incur additional expenses.

Apart from finances, the most frequently cited reason for staying in a home that one of the spouses lived in prior to the remarriage is not wanting to uproot children. "They've had to deal with so much already," Esther says of her three school-age children, who found themselves fatherless two years ago when her husband was killed in a car accident. "They're dealing fairly well with the prospect of my remarriage. I don't want to move them and ask them to adjust to yet another trauma. Not now."

Neutralizing the ground. However hard you try to block them out, ghosts of the past haunt the old residence.

A man moving into his new wife's home is told which closet is his — not because it's the one he wants but because it's the one the man of the house has always had.

A woman wants to move some of the objects her husband collected with a former wife. He objects.

A man discovers the mortgage payments on his wife's condo are being paid for, in part, by his wife's former husband, who is half owner of the place. He feels like a "kept" man.

A stepparent is turned into an intruder by the kids who have been living in the house. "Who does he think he is putting his desk into the den?" one angry stepson asks. "This is our house."

Countering the uncomfortable feelings of the newcomer and the proprietary feelings in-residence family members have when newcomers move in challenges the newly remarried couple's tact, sensitivity, and creativity.

What follows are stories from families who have done it and, in the process, discovered some ways to make the process of blending easier.

1. "Sid didn't like the idea of sleeping in the same room my former husband and I slept in — nor did I, frankly. But

what really jolted us into action was the fact that my daughter, Ellen, kept referring to our bedroom as 'yours and Daddy's room.' We renovated the attic of the house and made it into a little apartment for ourselves. Ellen was given the choice of staying in her old room or claiming the master bedroom. She chose the master bedroom and then painted and redecorated it. Her old room became the guest room her stepbrothers used when they visited. They were given the option to decorate that room any way they liked — within reason — and they plastered the walls with posters of their favorite rock stars."

Hints: *Shuffle bedrooms.* Bedrooms are the private areas in a home. Changing whose is whose makes you and the resident children feel like you're in a new place. It also helps to evict the ghosts.

Redecorate. Encourage children to redecorate too. Don't expect that children will bring the same taste to a bedroom that you will. But give them as much latitude as you can stomach (and afford) to make their bedrooms uniquely theirs.

2. In Marsha's separation agreement with her former husband, she had the right to live in the house until her son reached the age of 18 or until she remarried — whichever came first. At that time, the house had to be sold to a third party or she had to buy her first husband out. Marsha and her fiancé, Ray, wanted to stay in the house. It would be better for her daughter, Marsha reasoned. Ray liked the idea because the house was close to his former wife's home, where his children live for four of the seven days of the week. The other three days they were with him as part of his joint-custody arrangement. The same bus would be able to drop the children off at either of their parents' homes.

Ray gave Marsha the $40,000 she needed to buy her former husband's half of the house. A portion of it came from his savings; a portion of it was borrowed, using the house he owned jointly with his former wife as collateral.

HINT: *Assume a financial obligation for or buy into the house, if you're the newcomer.* Many divorce agreements state that one party, usually the wife, has the right to remain in the house until the kids are grown or until some other agreed-upon time, like the wife's remarriage. When one of those dates is triggered, the property is to be sold and the profits divided. A new husband, if he can afford it, can buy the former husband's half (either directly or indirectly, through his new wife). Even if he can't, he and his wife can take out a home equity loan to pay off the former husband.

Suppose one of the spouses owns the house outright. Then the other should take an active financial part in the upkeep of the residence. Perhaps it means writing out the mortgage check from one's own account or paying for the maintenance on the property. He or she *feels* a sense of ownership when the contribution is made. And indeed, the ownership would probably be viewed as real, if the couple were to separate and the matter went to court — even if the original owner's name remained on the existing deed.

3. "Without realizing it, I was always referring to the house as 'my house,' " Maddy confesses. "I'd tell people 'I' was putting an addition on 'my house.' Even though Paul was paying for it, I still felt in control. Paul felt it, too, because at a business dinner I said 'my house' once too often and Paul exploded. We had a terrible fight. I wasn't sensitive to the discomfort Paul felt about living here nor to his dislike over my possessiveness about the house I had lived in for thirteen years."

HINT: *Be alert to signs of any uneasiness your spouse might feel about this arrangement.* It isn't easy to be the outsider in someone else's home. Don't use the powerful situation to lessen the influence, responsibility, or decision-making capacity of your spouse. Learn to say "our home."

4. "I bought my dream house just months before the divorce from my second husband," Lynn says. "For the next

three years, while I was single again, I fixed it up just the way I wanted. Then I met Marvin. After his divorce he had bought a broken-down home with a lot of history behind it. Over the years he had renovated it and eventually gotten it on the historic register. He wanted me to move into his house. I wanted him to move into mine." It was, Lynn admits, the single most difficult issue they had to resolve when they married.

The compromise: Marvin moved in to Lynn's house, but he brought along his furniture.

HINT: *Compromise so that each of you has enough of yourself in this house to make you both feel at home.*

Merging Two Households

Is it because of this compromising that the "eclectic look" in household furnishing has become so popular? I wonder if it didn't jump into vogue when the divorce and remarriage rate skyrocketed.

Merging two disparate styles can make for a fascinating look. A Hoosier cabinet housing a compact disc player. A sleek leather sofa softened with needlepoint pillows. Currier and Ives prints grouped under halogen lighting.

Culling through the effects of two households to put together one exciting decor sounds intriguing. But even the most creative spirit finds it can be a nightmare. You have to work through your emotional connection to an object; your spouse must do the same. If there are children involved, you must tread delicately when assessing items they consider theirs — like VCRs, beds, or phones. To a child undergoing upheaval as a result of the remarriage, even the kitchen table becomes "mine" and an object to fight over. Children, especially, want to hang on to the familiar, the comfortable, and *most important*, the life *before* the stepparent. Respect that (even if it galls you). Prior to disposing of excess equipment, furniture, or appliances, give children who are old enough to make decisions a chance to sort through their own things, selecting what's meaningful to them and what they think they can part with.

Discard as much as possible before you make the actual move so you don't have to pay movers to tote items you're going to get rid of in a few months. Then dispose of unwanted items using any of the following unloading methods:

• Have a "cash and marry" garage sale and make some money from the duplicate items.

• Give the extras to relatives or to a charity. "It was harder to dispose of my period furniture than I thought it would be," Charlotte reports. "When I tried to entice my adult children into taking different pieces, each and every one told me that they didn't like French provincial. I was a bit taken aback — considering they had lived with this style for all the years they were growing up."

• Auction or sell to dealers pieces of worth.

• Put furniture in storage, saving it for children when they're old enough to move into quarters of their own or for a second home that you plan to buy one day.

Carla, an Atlanta copy editor, had another reason for renting storage space. "When Joel and I got married 11 years ago, we were in love but not in trust. That's why I put all the duplicate items I brought into the household — furniture, washing machine, mixer, even a toaster — into storage rather than selling or giving them away. I had been badly hurt in my first marriage — both emotionally and financially — and I wasn't giving up 'my' things easily. My fear was 'What if we get a divorce?' As I grew more confident about the relationship, I started to sell off things. About five years into the marriage, I was out of storage."

Carla concludes: "When we replaced our dressers with built-in cabinets, I knew our marriage was solid."

Chapter 5

ABCs of Money Management
Accounts, Budgets, and Chores

DID YOU KNOW . . .

- Among married couples, fewer women than men want to pool funds.
- Husbands and wives who do not believe that marriage should be forever are less willing to pool funds.
- Couples who fight about money argue more often about *how* it is to be spent than about *how much* they have to spend.
- Husbands and wives who feel they have equal control over how money is spent have a more tranquil relationship.

"In my first marriage, I controlled the money; she controlled the sex. Neither of us was happy," says Arnie, a Savannah, Georgia, CPA. "Now Jan manages some money, I manage some, and neither of us really knows how much we have left at the end of the month. But that's fine with me."

Sex aside for the moment, we do handle our finances differently in a remarriage than we did in the first go-around. There's more sharing when it comes to decision making. Women want more involvement this time and men appear more eager to give up some of the responsibility, according to a 1989 study conducted by Marilyn Coleman, Professor and Chair of the Department of Human Development and Family Studies, and Lawrence Ganong, Associate Professor in the School of Nursing, both at the University of Missouri.

Shared decision making bodes well for a remarriage. The sharing that happens as a result of positive communication should lessen the intensity and the frequency of money fights. I say "should" because sharing doesn't ensure tranquility. Increased financial responsibility and its inherent stress present a challenge to the balance of goodwill you will create by sharing.

"A" for Accounts

With the first electric bill (and right on through tuition invoices), who pays for what is an issue in remarriage.

Most remarrieds start with a set of pots. An unmatched set.

One pot is his. One pot is hers. One might be theirs. One might be hers with a child. Or his with a child.

They might have his and her business pots. Pots with parents. Trust pots. Even pots with former spouses.

For the sake of reducing the pot tally, let's limit discussion to what we could call the 1, 2, 3 Pot Remarriage system.

- The one-pot has all accounts (checking, savings, and investments) in joint names.
- The two-pot has all accounts divided (rarely evenly) into his accounts and her accounts.
- The three-pot has a his account, a her account, and a their account.

There's no right or wrong number of pots for a remarriage. You have to achieve a comfortable balance between your individual needs for independence and autonomy and commitment to the "common good" of the remarriage.

For Enid, a psychotherapist in Houston, and Dan, a manager in the international division of a Fortune 500 company, the two-pot set is a must. "It's definitely a what's-mine-is-mine; what's-yours-is-yours marriage," says Enid. "Not that we aren't both very generous to each other. We are. But I get pride out of handling my own finances and he feels the same way about his. If we had done that 'we' number, I would have become too vigilant about the way he spends money. I would be resentful when we spend large sums to bring his children up from Argentina twice a year.

"We've limited our financial expectations of each other. And therefore, we've limited our resentment."

Women, especially those who experience a precipitous drop in income after a divorce, are skittish about pooling funds. "I was so badly stung, financially, when Albert and I split," says Faith, "that I can't bear the idea of a joint account which Bernie, my new husband, might be able to raid. If I were perfectly honest, I suppose I'd have to call this my 'get up and go' account in case this marriage fails."

Sharon represents the other end of the comfort scale. An advertising account executive on parental leave caring for their two small boys, she has been living with Peter, an art director — in London, New York, and now Los Angeles — for the past 13 years, and married to him for nine. "We pooled our resources from the very beginning — even though Peter was in major hock, paying back all the debts from his past marriage. My small income was all we had."

Most remarrieds shift accounts from time to time simply because there's a difference in how you view your pot collection after 5 years of marriage, after 10, and after 20. Also, there's a difference in how you view it if you have a child together, when a weekend-visiting child becomes your permanent resident, and when all the children are grown.

The One-Pot System. Pooling all the income in a joint account from which expenses and investments are drawn seems to work best for young families with limited resources, for childless remarrieds, and for couples who have secure and long remarriages — so much so they can't even remember their "former lives." There is very little negotiating that has to be done with this arrangement. In remarried families where there are children, it has the psychological effect of saying that the money of the family is being committed to the common good of the family and without regard to who comes from which family. And with regard to the spouses, it indicates there is no one adult who wields the power over finances.

The Two-Pot System. Each of you keeps your income and accounts separate and each retains control over your own individual expenditures. It's pretty tough to figure out who used what electricity or to pluck numbers from the phone bill to assess whose long-distance calls were whose, so couples make accommodations. "The mortgage is your responsibility; utilities, mine." "Your children's room redecoration is yours; I'll pay for entertainment when my kids come visiting." Or they set up elaborate (and sometimes hysterically cumbersome) formulas. "Your two children live with us, but they only eat as much as one adult, so you should pay two thirds of the food costs; I'll pay one third. And because we have to cart them places frequently, I'll assume one quarter of the car costs, you handle the other three quarters."

Couples with this two-pot setup are usually more affluent, may be older when they remarry, or they have strong needs for personal autonomy. As a practical matter, if one of the spouses is heavily in debt when he or she remarries and fears not being able to pay the indebtedness off, then maintaining separate accounts insulates the mate from having assets attached.

Problems and resentments build when there is an inequality in income and one partner always winds up with a zero balance at the end of the month, while the other still has plenty to spend. If this happens, it's time to consider moving to three pots.

Spouses in two-pot families have less-positive feelings for their mates' children, the Coleman/Ganong study reports. Perhaps that's why the two accounts were established in the first place. Johnny's mom doesn't want her new husband looking over her shoulder questioning her generosity to her child. The problem is that by setting up the separate account, Johnny's mom frequently exacerbates her husband's resentment.

Does the two-pot system perpetuate divided loyalties? Probably. But it also offers autonomy and control to each spouse.

The Three-Pot System. The yours, mine, and ours system of managing income and expenses is designed to bolster commitment by emphasizing the needs of the family as a whole while also allowing each of you the freedom of a private fund. Each family puts its own spin on this system when it decides which items will be paid for individually and which jointly — and how much from each spouse's paycheck will go into each fund.

You can go about this one of two ways.

1. Pool all resources initially to pay for joint expenses and then withdraw money for your own personal accounts (see p. 77).

2. Put your paycheck into your own account and from that allocate a portion into a joint account (see p. 78). You need to agree on what proportion of each paycheck will be put into your joint account.

Although some remarrieds will, over a period of years, move on to a single-pot system, most remain with some adaptation of the three-pot system. It seems to encompass the best of all worlds for people who want some autonomy but whose conversation is sprinkled with "we's."

"In the early stages of our marriage, we were dogmatic

ONE SOLUTION FOR REMARRIEDS WITH CHILDREN

HIS INCOME	HER INCOME
Salary, investments, windfall	Salary, investments, windfall, child support payments from former husband

JOINT FUND
- Rent/mortgage
- Household expenses
- Entertainment for family
- US entertainment
- Food
- All car expenses and purchases
- All needs of children living in household
- His/her doctor bills
- Savings for emergency accounts and investments
- His/her fund contributions — a set $ amount

HIS FUND
- Alimony to former wife
- Child support for children living with former wife
- Gifts for his children and family
- Season tickets to Redskins games
- Clothes for himself
- Miscellaneous personal expenses

HER FUND
- Gifts for her children and family
- Clothes for herself
- Tennis club membership
- Miscellaneous personal expenses

ANOTHER SOLUTION FOR REMARRIEDS WITH CHILDREN

HIS INCOME	HER INCOME
Salary, investments, windfall	Salary, investments, windfall, child support payments from former husband

HIS FUND

- Alimony
- Child support
- Gifts for his children and family
- Personal expenses
- Clothes for himself
- His doctor bills
- Upkeep on his car
- Savings for his child's college
- Hobbies and collections
- Joint fund — 40% of income

HER FUND

- Gifts for her children and family
- Clothes for herself
- Health club
- Personal expenses
- Her doctor bills
- Savings for her children's college
- Joint fund — 50% of income

JOINT FUND

- Rent/mortgage
- Family car
- Entertainment for family
- US entertainment
- Household expenses
- Food
- All needs of children living in household
- Savings for emergency accounts and investments

about keeping our finances separate," Carla says of her 14-year marriage to Dennis, who had been married before. "We kept telling each other that we were totally committed to the marriage because we equated commitment with fidelity. But without realizing it, we held back. Not sexually. Monetarily. It wasn't until we opened up a joint account, about six years after we were married, that we fully understood what the word 'commitment' meant."

B for Budgetview

Ban the "B" word if when you hear it you think of deprivation, restriction, limits, quotas, and martyrdom. But when you want to buy a new car and need to find the money for it, or want to take the *whole* family on vacation and have to determine whether you need to sell stock to finance it, do a "Budgetview" — which is really a spending plan. (Cash analysis sounds like you're in a business together, but that's probably not how you're operating.)

In a Budgetview you look at the situation as if you were peering down at a chessboard. You can assess where the pieces are and you can move them — to fit your own family's needs. You plan for the long term, but since you never know the next move life is going to make, you remain flexible.

Most appealing about a Budgetview is that when you're all finished you don't try to squeeze yourself into someone else's assessment of how things ought to be. Remarried and stepfamilies aren't like others. There are financial pulls and pushes that nuclear families don't experience. So you have to create oddball financial plans that are molded around quickie weekends at romantic inns that coincide with a child's visit to a noncustodial parent, reupholstering the furniture of a "former life" to match new tastes, and astronomical long-distance phone charges (to stay close to children who don't live with you).

Placing the pieces. How much are you earning and how much are you spending? Most people know *approximately* what they earn (thanks to the IRS's forcing an assessment each April). But few people could come within a couple thousand dollars of what they really spend, if they were simply to guess. This is true in any relationship; it's especially true in a remarriage. This new union is not accustomed to the expenses that aren't listed in traditional budgets: children's travel expenses when they visit noncustodial parents; entertainment when they visit you; expenses agreed to under a separation agreement; additional gifts as a result of having a swollen family tree or guilt over divorcing a child's mother. An auctioneer from Kansas City was dumbfounded when he went back over his checkbook to calculate just how much he had spent during the past year on his two teenage children, who were living with their mother in the same city. "Under my separation agreement," he relates, "I must pay $15,000 a year support. In reality, when you count the hockey uniforms, braces for my daughter's teeth, Christmas, birthday, and what I call 'guilt-driven' presents, I spent $31,000 on my children."

Do you know how much you spend a year? Do you know how much you as a couple spend? Without going back to the checkbook or canceled checks, guesstimate how much your annual expenses are.

Guesstimate of Your Annual Expenses $———

There are now two ways to determine if you are anywhere near the actual amount.

The first way, the "Get It Over With" estimate, can be done one rainy Saturday — but the picture it provides is fuzzy.

The second, the "Document Your Life" method, provides a sharper image but requires diligence in recording everything you spend over a three-month period.

For people who don't have a long history together —

those who are just getting married or in the first year of a remarriage — the slow, tiresome "Document Your Life" method makes more sense because your financial life together is still an unknown adventure.

For remarrieds with a year or more behind them, the "Get It Over With" estimate — rough as it is — is adequate, especially if you're an impatient sort who disdains detail and will forget to write down each expenditure.

Whichever method you choose (and ultimately your decision will be based on your psyche and available time), it's important to know what you're spending. Without that knowledge, you can't adequately plan for what you want as a person, as a couple, and as a family.

The "Document Your Life" Method. Since your work will extend over a three-month period, make life simple for yourself. Keep as little cash in your pocket as possible and pay for almost everything by check or with a credit card. That includes meals out, commutation tickets, childcare expenses, cleaning, even groceries. That way, when you get your canceled checks (even if you forget to record the check) and your credit card bills, you'll have a record of what you spent for what. And the unaccounted cash you've withdrawn from the bank or the automatic teller machines (which will show up on your bank statements) can be slotted into the PERSONAL column without guilt that you should have put it elsewhere but can't remember where.

Once a month, pull together the following items:

1. the past month's
    - canceled checks
    - bank statements
    - credit card statements
    - pay stubs, investment and dividend income stubs, child support/alimony totals, any income documentation from rental properties,

sale of assets, trusts, unemployment, or disability

2. a calculator (If this is an exercise you think you'll want to engage in regularly or if you want to monitor your finances, consider buying one of the many comprehensive personal finance computer programs available, such as *Managing Your Money* or *Quicken*).

3. a notebook or the back of your datebook in which you have recorded miscellaneous expenditures.

Figure on spending a couple of hours together each month, entering the numbers. Don't try to analyze them. That will come later.

The "Get It Over With" Estimate. Gather up:

1. last year's
   - canceled checks
   - credit card statements
   - bank statements (for money taken out of the cash machine and from the teller)
   - tax return (to find out how much you earned and from what sources)

2. a calculator.

Set aside five to six hours to figure out what you spent last year. If you're doing this prior to your remarriage, you have to do it separately and then merge the two lists — guessing what the joint figure will be, since, obviously, it won't be the sum of both your individual expenses. Nor will it be particularly accurate. Even if you've been remarried for years, you'll have to do a lot of guessing since you really can't be sure how much of the $100 that you took out of the automatic teller machine on July 5 was for cleaning, ice cream, a gift, a phone, or something you've long since forgotten.

The "Get It Over With" estimate is best done right around tax time. After all, you have all your financial records out anyway.

The Worksheet. The worksheets on the following pages will work whichever method you opt for. If you do the three-month "Document Your Life" analysis, there's a possibility you might not choose a period during which large bills come due, such as a life insurance or auto insurance premium. If that's the case, just note it under the onetime expense column.

You will note one worksheet item that is not usually on an expense analysis. It's "US." Remarriages need nurturing. And in the midst of mounting emotional and financial pressures from relatives and friends, nurturing the relationship often gets slighted. Don't let it happen. The studies and observations of all those who have studied remarriage, including Drs. Emily and John Visher, cofounders of the Stepfamily Association of America, reveal that remarriages are successful only if the couple has developed a solid couple bond. It's not only important for you, but it also makes for a smoother family life (although the children may resent it at first). Setting time and money aside for time alone is an essential expense.

BUDGETVIEW

EXPENSES

Item	Jan.		Feb.		Mar.		Apr.		May		June	
	H	W	H	W	H	W	H	W	H	W	H	W
BASIC HOUSING (Your rent/mortgage; taxes; insurance; utilities, such as gas, water, sewer, fuel; telephone)												
HOUSING UPKEEP (Repairs, home improvements, furniture, equipment, appliances, cable, household help)												
FOOD (Your total grocery bill plus the meals you eat out)												
CLOTHING (What you buy as well as what you spend on upkeep, such as cleaning and repairs)												
TRANSPORTATION (Everything you spend for your car[s] — upkeep, gas, insurance, fees, parking, monthly loan repayment. If you buy a new car outright every 5 years, for example, divide the real cost —the cost of the new car minus what you get when you trade in or sell the old one — by 5 and put the figure in the onetime-expense column for the year. Add your bus, train, taxi expenses — and any other expenses connected to commuting. Add children's travel.)												

ly	Aug.		Sept.		Oct.		Nov.		Dec.		Onetime Expense	
W	H	W	H	W	H	W	H	W	H	W	Husband	Wife

Item	Jan.		Feb.		Mar.		Apr.		May		Jur
	H	W	H	W	H	W	H	W	H	W	H
EDUCATION (Tuition and all other expenses for private schools, colleges, courses, seminars; books, news-papers, magazines)											
MEDICAL (The difference between what your insurance covers and what you spend for doctors, hospitals, drugs, and other medical services and products for yourselves and all the children you have finan-cial responsibility for; insur-ance — life, medical, disability — premiums)											
FAMILY (Childcare; child support/ alimony payments; allowances and other money given to chil-dren directly; family entertain-ment, vacations, and recreation)											
US (Travel, vacation, entertainment for the two of you)											
SAVINGS AND INVESTMENTS (All pension plan contributions, such as IRAs, 401(k)s; all other — including fund contri-butions, real estate investments, etc.)											
CHARITY AND GIFTS (Wedding, birthday, Christmas and Hanukkah presents; charita-ble contributions you've written out in check form; what you con-tribute that's unaccounted for)											

uly	Aug.		Sept.		Oct.		Nov.		Dec.		Onetime Expense	
W	H	W	H	W	H	W	H	W	H	W	Husband	Wife

Item	Jan.		Feb.		Mar.		Apr.		May		Jun	
	H	W	H	W	H	W	H	W	H	W	H	
DEBT (All interest and principal you're paying on loans other than auto and mortgage, including what you owe as a result of a former marriage)												
TAXES (What you paid in federal, state, and local taxes last year. Tally up what was withheld, what you paid in estimated taxes, and what you paid when you filed your return. If money was refunded to you, subtract that from the total.)												
PERSONAL (AND OFTEN UNTRACEABLE) (The money you put into your pocket each day that frequently just disappears. You have to guess at this.)												
TOTALS												

If you've done the 3-month analysis, multiply your 3-month totals by 4 and then add your onetime expense column to your total expenditures.

If you've done last year's analysis, add all the monthly columns (you shouldn't have anything under the onetime expense column) for your total expenditures.

ly	Aug.		Sept.		Oct.		Nov.		Dec.		Onetime Expense	
W	H	W	H	W	H	W	H	W	H	W	Husband	Wife

How Close Were You? Look back to your guesstimate of your yearly expenses. If the calculations put you within 10% of the estimate, congratulate yourself. You have a real handle on your personal finances. Most of us underestimate our expenses by at least 20%.

BUDGETVIEW

INCOME

Source	Jan.		Feb.		Mar.		Apr.		May		Ju
	H	W	H	W	H	W	H	W	H	W	H
Salary, wages, tips											
Bonus											
Profit-sharing											
Interest & dividends											
Proceeds from											
sale of securities											
Rental income											
Income from											
trusts, estates											
Social Security											
Pension											
Disability											
Child support											
Windfall											
or inheritance											
Other											

If you've done the three-month analysis of your income, multiply the three-month totals and add your onetime income to get your total annual income.

Now see how your income stacks up with your expenses.

ANNUAL INCOME $_____

ANNUAL EXPENSES $_____

ly	Aug.		Sept.		Oct.		Nov.		Dec.		Onetime Expense	
W	H	W	H	W	H	W	H	W	H	W	Husband	Wife

Remember expenditures change. Yes, it's possible (even probable) that your former spouse will remarry and you'll be spared alimony payments, or that your son will come live with you and your new spouse and your former spouse will refuse to contribute to his support. You might have children of your own. The shifting households of remarried families and the passage of time make change inevitable. But that's when the initial Budgetview takes on the greatest importance. Having the picture planted on paper allows you to move the pieces with more confidence. If you know you'll be saving $5,000 annually on alimony, you'll be able to allocate that money to another category — entertainment, family, savings. If you're aware that having another child in the household will mean an additional $5,800 the first year, you'll have a better idea of where to move money from.

The "B" word resurfaces. If you can remember that budgets are made to fit people and not the other way around, you won't gag on the "B" word. But saying it doesn't mean you have to put it down on paper. Once you've done the Budgetview, most people can figure out how they're doing — expenses versus income — without keeping a running written record. I know I risk scorn from financial planners of the type-A variety, but unless there is some dramatic change in circumstances or your expenses-to-income ratio is in terminal imbalance, you don't have to do the Budgetview more than once every couple of years. Formal, annual reports to yourself are good only if they make you feel more comfortable. If they loom like monsters, skip a year. And once you've been married for a few years, you'll be able to predict with some accuracy the changes that will be occurring (such as the end of *formal* support payments or the beginning of support responsibilities for an elderly parent) and adjust to them.

If the bottom line of expense to income is out of whack and there doesn't seem to be a way you can live year to year without gnawing at savings or getting into debt, you'll find strategies for reversing the flow in the next chapter, "When There's Not Enough."

C for Chores

Financial decision making should be shared.

But who pays the bills, fills out the forms for a mutual fund account, gets the papers ready for the accountant, fights with Visa over a bill? Well, that's another matter.

Forget gender. Who likes to do those tasks? If you both do, split them up or take turns — switching every six months. If one of you has an accountant's love for detail and wouldn't miss a reconciliation session with a bank statement for all the chips in tollhouse cookies, bless him or her.

But if the chores have fallen, by default, to one of you who has little time or love for them, be creative in your approach to the task. Options include:

1. Calculating how many hours a week it takes to keep the family finances under control, and trading off some of your other responsibilities with your spouse (such as mowing the lawn, picking the children up from Sunday school, or grocery shopping).

2. Paying yourself for the chore with time alone — and letting your spouse know that that's what you're doing so he or she can take over parenting or housekeeping chores during that time.

3. Devising the simplest financial record–keeping system you can, because if you feel overwhelmed or if your expensive, sophisticated, precise computer system has too long a learning curve, you'll lose interest and do nothing.

4. Practicing one of the following chore-dodging ploys that either shortens the length of time on task or eliminates it altogether. (And don't let anyone make you feel guilty. Bankers, lawyers, and CPAs do it.) Ploys include:

- Not balancing your checkbook. Or at least not doing it every month. Heresy, you say. Why? Is it really important to know to the penny how much you have? If you can't keep a fairly accurate running total in your head, call the bank or punch into the automatic teller machine once in a while to find out what's left in the account. Two precautionary measures in case your mental math fails: pad your account with a $100 unrecorded deposit and set up an overdraft account, really a line of credit. The one chore you must do: record all deposits.

- Rounding checks and balances in your checkbook up to the nearest dollar. Who needs to spend time adding up pennies? This ploy also gives you a tiny financial cushion against error.
- Closing your account and starting again. This is akin to having your house repainted when the task of washing the walls seems too overwhelming.
- Hiring someone to take care of your finances. You don't have to be mentally incompetent to cry for help. One couple says that hiring a financial manager literally saved their marriage because they no longer fight over who does what and have more quality time together.

Which brings us back to the opening passage in this chapter — sex in Arnie's remarriage.

"As for sex," Arnie adds as postscript, "we manage it as a team." Just as money should be managed.

Chapter 6

When There's Not Enough

DID YOU KNOW . . .
- After a divorce, women and their children suffer a 73% drop in standard of living, while their former husbands enjoy a gain of 42% in theirs.
- Children get 2% more expensive to support each year.
- The majority of stepfamilies are at an economic disadvantage relative to other family types. Median family income for all married-couple family households in 1985 was $28,162, according to a Census Bureau study. Families consisting of a stepfather and a biological mother had a median family income of $25,272.
- Families in which there are one or more stepchildren plus an "ours" child have the lowest median income: $22,932.
- Families with a stepmother and a biological father have the highest median family income: $34,850.
- When a husband and wife are disappointed with the amount of money they have, they find their whole relationship less satisfying.

"There comes a time early in the month when you feel that you are not going to make it through February," writes columnist Russell Baker of the gloom of winter. But the beginning-of-the-month blues would be just as apt if he were talking about the money woes of remarried families.

Even today, when both husband and wife are likely to work, remarried households with children living at home are the worst off, economically, relative to other married-family types.

Financial strains common in remarriages aren't calibrated just on how much the couple earns. How much financial pressure the couple feels is also part of the measurement. When you live up to what you earn (and most people do), you feel all the money earned is needed. Suppose, for example, an annual household income is $85,000 and $15,000 of that has always been used for child support. When that support obligation ceases, the unshackled $15,000 is used to buy a much-needed car or fund a retirement plan. It's rarely spent on a Christian Dior original or dinners out for the next year. With the exception of the very wealthy, people always have a "need" for money, though needs change. And it's ridiculous to get into a contest over who has the greatest need — even though you always have to make decisions about allocating resources. Is a stepchild's private-school need greater than your need for a vacation? Or is your need for a new suit less meaningful than your spouse's need to join a health spa? These are personal decisions, of course, to be made on a case-by-case basis.

Pair ongoing money squeezes with the financial emergencies that may strike any family from time to time and problems compound. One of you is fired or unable to work for an extended time; the family is hit with an enormous, unexpected expense. How do you handle the times of trouble? The defensive and offensive strategies that follow will help. But as a government official said of the year he was out of work as a result of a layoff, grit and a supportive spouse are the secrets to getting through the tough times. "If Molly had been the same type as my former wife, I probably would have hung myself by now. But her optimistic attitude, quiet pullback in spending, and constant encouragement helped me pull through."

The Ongoing Squeeze

Dick, a San Diego–based marketing manager, visualizes the financial pressures of supporting two families this way. "It's as if a hose were attached to my checking account, steadily drawing out money." He's at the point that whenever he writes a check that's not part of his fixed expenses, he tenses up, certain he'll go into debt. To his first family, he's legally bound; to his second, he feels financially strapped.

Children are squeezes extraordinaire. They are more expensive than statistics indicate, especially in upper-income families where the parents are eager to give children more — more education, more lessons, more clothes, more material goods. And children, whether hers, his, or theirs, give the word "unforeseen" an expensive cast. Unforeseen natural ability as a golfer, for example, puts pressure on parents and stepparents to buy equipment and pay for transportation to and from amateur tournaments. Unforeseen injuries, doctors' bills, or special needs shadow children at different times in their growing-up years.

State laws generally relieve stepparents of the financial responsibility for their stepchildren, except when the children are, or are about to become, public charges. The primary financial responsibility is on the biological parents. But real life isn't that neat. You marry someone. Your lives entwine. Even if you try to insulate yourself, you find yourself feeling somewhat responsible for your stepchildren. As time goes on, you might grow to love them. And then the question is not who's responsible for what, but what can you afford and what do you want to do for the children.

When there's not enough money, resentment can erupt. Often one partner feels too much of the joint funds are being used to meet the financial needs of a prior marriage. Worse still is when a new spouse feels his or her personal funds are being drained by the obligations of the other spouse.

Stepfathers, especially, get tapped. They frequently are asked to contribute to stepchildren's financial well-being when a wife's former husband skips out on support. (The errant parent rationalizes it this way: "My former wife has remarried. Now let someone else foot the bills." Unfortunately, too many fathers feel this way — perhaps they're jealous of a new man usurping their role in their children's lives.)

Stepmothers who are financially independent and bring no children of their own to the new marriage frequently find themselves contributing to the support of a former wife who refuses to work or can't. Says an ad-agency executive who buys clothes for her two stepchildren every time they visit: "I hate that woman [the children's mother]. She sends the kids to us in clothes two sizes too small and tells them to ask us for clothes because she doesn't have enough money to buy them herself. Considering what my husband gives her for support, her actions are appalling. I end up paying for everything in our marriage because most of what he makes goes to kids. As a result, though we should have bought a condo a long time ago, we're still renting."

The squeeze continues and resentment boils when a husband or wife feels the former spouse isn't participating in the support of children. "My former wife has made an art of avoiding full-time remunerative employment," Dennis complains bitterly. "If she earned *anything*, she'd take some of the pressure off me." Says Dennis's second wife, a successful magazine editor with no children of her own, "On a good day in a good year, I don't mind chipping in or having Dennis contribute most of his earnings to care for his children and first wife. We have always had enough. But this year is a shaky one for both of us. I'm annoyed that Dennis doesn't say something to force her into taking a job and contributing to the kids' support."

When can you tell that the financial strain is too great?

Warning Signs

Recognizing early signs of trouble and responding to them swiftly is the best defense against months that stretch further than a paycheck. The financial squeeze is on when you

- feel as if you're losing control of your life
- use your savings to pay current expenses
- postdate checks to keep them from bouncing
- send less support/alimony than you are obligated to, are constantly late with it, or fail to send it altogether
- continually dip into the credit line of your checking account
- regularly exceed the borrowing limit on your credit cards
- use cash advances from some credit cards to pay off others
- pay only the minimum balance due on credit cards
- borrow money from friends and relatives for current expenses

What can you do to ease the financial pressure?

Remarrieds have the same fiscal choice as others caught in a financial vise: spend less or earn more. They also have the recourse of going after a parent who is not providing the agreed-upon support. Support-payers can cut the outflow by reducing support.

Spend Less

Clearly the first step for chronically overspending couples is an analysis of their Budgetview with an eye to shaving expenses in nonessential areas. Spending cuts should be a joint task. No one person should be the martyr, sacrificing his or her comforts or resources for the good of everyone else. Martyrs aren't loved. Who wants to crawl into bed with a haloed spouse?

Each partner must review his or her own expenditures, making reductions that reflect individual priorities. Dick said he was willing to brown-bag lunch a few times a week but couldn't bear forgoing his health club membership, which was reasonably priced by neighborhood standards. His wife felt her fashionable haircut couldn't be done by anyone but her expensive stylist, but she could give up the weekly manicure.

Decisions on joint expenses are up for discussion and negotiation. Examine each section of the Budgetview for a possible reduction of living expenses. If the imbalance of income to expenses is only slight, simple fine-tuning is all you need: postponing the purchase of a new car for another year, eating one less meal out every week, or giving less-elaborate gifts to each other or family members. Facing a problem together and finding creative solutions can defuse the feelings of despair or helplessness and give more padding to the middle ground needed for a successful remarriage.

Instead of being ushered to a posh restaurant table once a week, Dick and Donna, for example, have found more ingenious and less-costly ways to be alone. They pack a wacky combination of childhood favorite foods and drive to the coast, where they watch the sun set as they down fluffernutter sandwiches, Malomar cookies, and milk. When possible, they exchange baby-sitting time with another couple and stay home — quietly.

10 Easy, Efficient "Get Smart" Ideas

Investigate these ideas immediately. (They're valuable even if you don't need to prune expenses.)

Insurance

1. Chip away at your car insurance premium. Quiz your agent about ways to lower the premium: higher deductible; installation of alarm systems, air bags; discounts for good driving and child-driver away at school; elimination of collision coverage on an old car.

2. Take advantage of your universal life policy. If you've been paying premiums regularly, this is the time to cash in on the flexibility of the policy by using your cash reserve. Check your yearly statement or call your broker to find out if you have enough in reserve to do this without affecting the amount of your coverage.

Credit

3. Empty your wallet or purse of credit cards. Pay off the outstanding balances on all but two of the cards, which you can put back in your wallet for emergency use. With your final payment to the credit card company, send a note saying you no longer want the card and return the two halves you've scissored. Savings accrue immediately. No more yearly fees on those cards.

4. Search for a bank card with an interest rate lower than what you're now paying. You might have to pay an annual fee of $25 or $50, but even that will be considerably lower than the monthly interest charges on a running balance of $1,000. Check monthly personal finance magazines like *Kiplinger's Personal Finance* or *Money* for banks with low interest rates on credit card balances.

Taxes and Financial Services

5. Do your own returns. Few items in the most recent tax legislation will affect how you fill out your return, so with last year's return at hand, do this year's — aided by one of the annual, step-by-step tax guides by J. K. Lasser, H&R Block, or Arthur Young, available in bookstores at the end of January. Even the IRS's free booklet "Your Federal Income Tax" will help. (Don't forget: the parent with physical custody for the greater portion of the year has the right to list children as dependents, even though he or she may not provide the majority of the support. For the IRS to recognize a different arrangement, the custodial parent must sign a form waiving his or her right to the exemption. The form then must be attached to the other parent's tax return.)

6. *Don't pay for what you can get for free.* Many financial services are free: no-fee checking accounts, no-load mutual funds, credit cards (although if you run a balance, your primary consideration has to be the rate of interest charged).

7. *Use money market accounts and funds for bills over $250.* If you're keeping the money you need for monthly expenditures in a no-interest checking account or a NOW account that earns a paltry return, transfer some money to a money market account at your bank (most allow you to write at least three large checks a month without charge) or a money market fund at a mutual fund (most have a dollar minimum of $250, but no minimum on the number of checks you write). That way you'll be earning interest while the money is waiting to be paid out.

Spending

8. *Quit carrying your ATM card.* If it's not in your wallet, you aren't tempted to drop into the bank to withdraw money. That, in turn, helps reduce impulse buying. Take as much from your paycheck as you will need until the next pay period. Spend only what you have in your wallet.

9. *Eliminate all (but the absolutely necessary) major expenses this year.* Pamper your old car and learn to live with less-than-state-of-the-art stereo components.

10. *Stop saving.* Sounds like strange advice, but this is not

the time to worry about contributing to a company retirement plan to save on taxes. Your first goal is to bring your day-to-day expenses in line.

Earn More

Even in tough financial times, careers flourish. Be aware of the possible areas of promotion within your own company and stay in touch with associates throughout the industry with an eye to spotting an opportunity for advancement that would carry with it a hike in salary.

What about the added income from moonlighting? A second job sounds like a sensible idea when a couple is strapped, but for couples in the early stages of a remarriage, it can be threatening. Time as a couple and time as a family are as precious as money for a new marriage. Weigh your answers to these questions before tackling another job.

• Will being away from each other (or the family) be more of a strain than cutting back on expenditures? Consider that others in the family might have to pick up additional responsibilities as a result of one of the adults being away more. Too, there is less time together; less time to develop a common middle ground and less time to meet the emotional needs of the members of this new family.

• Can the drain on your time and energy be limited? Can you moonlight just long enough to tide you over a rough spot or must you do this for as long as you can foresee?

• How will the extra income affect your taxes?

• What are the additional costs (transportation; clothes; meals out; payment for home services such as housework, gardening, maintenance, and repair work now done by one of the spouses; childcare) associated with earning this extra income?

• Can you start a small business from your home that allows you to work together? For couples in the early stages of a remarriage who need to nurture the relationship, turning a hobby or service into additional income can be fun and profitable "togetherness." Children can be brought in to help, giving them a sense of belonging to this new family unit.

Starting a venture is risky business, as everyone knows. So be certain the business you're contemplating will be as investment- and risk-free as possible — perhaps a much-needed service you can provide comfortably without an infusion of capital. Self-employeds have many tax breaks — not the least of which is being able to deduct expenses for that portion of your home used exclusively for business.

Reduce Support for Children from a Former Marriage

It sounds heartless and sometimes it is. But not always. Suppose the company you work for closes its doors — no warning, no severance, no benefits. It happens. Even though your former spouse would probably challenge it, you could argue that if you were not divorced and remarried, your first family would still have to cut back its spending and retrench because of this situation.

If you petition the court to modify alimony and/or support payments for your noncustodial children, you might win. You usually must prove there's been a substantial change in your financial position — one that was not anticipated when the original payments were set. States vary in how they view remarriage when considering a reduction in support payments. Most deny modification simply because a noncustodial parent remarries, holding that earlier obligations come first — an approach that's been called "vasectomy by dollar bill."

Though it may be absolutely necessary, the decision to seek reduction of support should never be made lightly. Emotional ramifications resound — even when the reduction is reasonable and appropriate to the circumstances. More often than not, children see it as further abandonment; former spouses use it to reemphasize the unworthiness of the noncustodial parent.

And it's costly. You wind up spending thousands on legal fees, money that could otherwise be provided for support or for righting your own financial position.

Just because a child switches households and comes to live with you and your new spouse, don't assume the court will permit a reduction in child support to your former wife for the other children. A father of three tells this story. "When my oldest child, Margie, came to live with us, I thought it was perfectly reasonable to ask my former wife to voluntarily agree to a reduction in child support. She didn't. Was I angry! I got a lawyer and appealed to the court. But because my income had risen since the separation agreement was signed six years before, the court didn't think a reduction was appropriate. I lost the appeal. And probably should have. I used the support issue to infuriate my former wife because I can't stand her."

Other states, other judges, might have made different determinations. Some do consider the expenses of second families, the contribution of the new spouse to those expenses, the support given to stepchildren, or any increased ability of the custodial parent to assume more of the financial responsibility.

Flush Out the Errant Parent

Child support isn't an issue that can be argued. Parents who sign separation agreements pledging a certain level of support (and even those who don't) are responsible for financial support — unless there is some good reason why they can't provide it.

If you have a noncustodial parent who neglects or disregards his or her parental responsibility, you have two courses of action. You can hire an attorney and bring the case to court or you can apply for child support enforcement (CSE) services. The private attorney route is more expensive (and when the shortage of money is a problem, cost is an important consideration).

Child support enforcement (CSE) legislation operates on federal and state levels. At the federal level, it is administered by the Office of Child Support Enforcement (OCSE). At the state level, responsibility may be in any local agency, but most frequently it's found in the social services or human resources department. Once you have contacted the division that handles child support enforcement in your state, you can go one of two routes — through the courts or through an administrative process. The courts offer a wider range of enforcement remedies, such as civil contempt and possible jail terms for the errant parent. The administration process offers quicker service and is less costly because you don't have court costs or attorney fees. CSE can enforce payment by seizing wages, imposing liens, intercepting state tax refunds, making the delinquency known to any consumer credit bureau asking for the information, and allowing the federal government to garnish wages, pension benefits, and retirement pay (including Social Security). Be forewarned, however. While child support receives some emphasis, states' efforts mainly have been on behalf of children who are or who are about to become public charges.

It's important to remember that all fathers who don't pay support on time or as much as they should aren't deadbeats. Jarvis, an engineer in Houston, is such a case. He was sued by his former wife because he was $900 behind in support, even though he told her he and his wife both had lost their jobs (within three months of each other) and that he'd be reducing support for his six-year-old son until he could find another position. Then he would make up the deficit, he said. Although his former wife was remarried and living in her new husband's home, she proceeded with court action. The outcome: Jarvis had to pay his attorney $2,800 and an extra $100 a month toward arrearages. "That wiped out half of our savings," he said. She paid her attorney $750. "Had she ridden out the hard times with me," he continued, "we both would have benefited — not the lawyers."

Times of Trouble

"One month before our marriage and after we closed on a house that we (and four children — two of hers and two of mine) were going to be living in, my company laid off half its employees. I was one of them," says Evan, an Augusta, Georgia, CPA. "We went ahead with our wedding plans because we figured Alice's position as assistant controller for a medium-sized company was secure, I would be employed shortly, and we both had houses to sell that we figured would go quickly and net us substantial profits.

"It took me much longer to get a job than I had anticipated: 10 months. The real estate market collapsed almost immediately and our respective homes are still on the market — 20 months later. Other than the fact that Alice is still working, this has been a financial nightmare."

If you have some warning. Sometimes you *see* the possibility of financial danger: You're having a child and know that for a year or two you're going to be living on one income. Or one of you is in the process of making a career change that is certain to cause a blip in income.

Sometimes you *sense* it. You know the company president and treasurer are closeted in meetings and there's a rumor your company is on the verge of bankruptcy. Or your former husband's regular support check comes later and later each month and is less than it should be.

If you see or sense trouble, take preventive measures immediately.

• *Do everything you would do if you were in a budget squeeze.* Ferret out the "must spends" — rent or mortgage, utilities, food, support/alimony. Create a "Crisis Budgetview" and follow it.

• *Establish a line of credit.* Apply for a home equity loan which you can tap into if needed. The interest payments are tax-deductible.

• *Make certain your assets are liquid.* That way, you can sell them easily if you have to. Don't put any new money into certificates of deposit (CDs), which penalize you for early withdrawals, or into real estate, which is difficult to sell on short notice. And if you do have extra funds now, make certain they're in income-oriented liquid investments.

When crisis blindsides you. You walk into your office anticipating the day ahead and your supervisor tells you the boss's nephew is replacing you. You must be out by 5:00 P.M.

Your spouse and stepchildren are in a terrible car accident. Medical insurance will only cover 80% of the bills. Your spouse will be out of work for at least six months and will need home care that must be paid for out-of-pocket.

Here's how to move on a dime to minimize the financial damage.

• *Do everything you would have done had you seen it coming.*

• *Call creditors and refinance or renegotiate loans.* While it's tempting to hope creditors won't notice you're in arrears, they do. Before you get the disconnect notice from the phone company, call and write to explain the problem. Most companies will accommodate you by accepting partial payment, converting you to a balanced billing system that spreads payments out equally over the year, or rescheduling the date you receive your bill. With a large debt, such as a car loan, some creditors will agree to stretch out your loan, thus reducing the monthly payments. The rationale behind the creditor's apparent largess: A payment in hand, even a partial payment, often is better than standing in the bankruptcy bushes trying to retrieve what's owed.

One writer whose book advance didn't stretch as long as

his auto loan payments was able to renegotiate his loan. Knowing he would be getting a substantial sum when the manuscript was accepted, he made a deal with the bank that required him to pay interest only until the single balloon payment of principal came due at the end of the loan period, which was a few months after he received the lump-sum payment for the book.

• *Call the institution holding your mortgage.* Banks are not eager to foreclose on one more piece of property that could be hard to unload. So let your bank know your problem. Together you might be able to work out a temporary solution, perhaps reduced payments drawn out over a longer period.

Having no choice but to close their scuba equipment store, a remarried couple was able to convince the savings and loan institution holding the mortgage on their house to suspend payments for a few months, giving them an opportunity to find jobs, which they did rather quickly. (In fact, the Florida savings and loan even put them in touch with a distributor who eventually bought their inventory.) If you're renting, try to strike a deal with your landlord. In some cities eviction is a long process that landlords would rather not go through, especially when they're dealing with well-meaning tenants who are going through hard times.

• *Involve all members of all families.* First, try to renegotiate support/alimony obligations with a former spouse. If you have a civil relationship and your position is clear and just, she or he may be willing to agree to a temporary reduction of support or alimony rather than run the risk of having nothing and then having to start legal proceedings to retrieve the obligation. Said one San Francisco woman about her former husband's bankruptcy, "What can I do? He's distraught about the failure of his bookshop. He's a good father, even if he was a lousy husband. I know he'll start the child support again as soon as he gets on his feet. Until then, my husband and I will take over the full support of the kids. We're lucky. We're in a position to do that without much problem."

Second, if you're the custodial parent and the one in the bind and have reason to believe the support you're receiving from your children's other parent can be increased, ask him or her for it — on a temporary basis. Sometimes, it's even possible to negotiate some future benefit, such as agreeing to give him more than one half of the proceeds from a jointly owned house that you will sell at some later date in exchange for more support now.

Third, talk to the children — those living with you and those who depend on you for support. Children are likely to be confused and resentful during this stressful period. They may even think they're causing the problems. Without scaring them or making them feel responsible for coming up with solutions, discuss the situation. An upstate New York high school administrator tells of the time, shortly after his remarriage, that he told his teenage children and stepchildren that he was resigning as principal of a school because he felt the situation in the community was intolerable. He explained the politics and principles behind his reasoning and then clarified how the decision would impact on the family. "I told them all that though I was a bit anxious, I was fully confident things would be resolved shortly. Until then, though, we would cut back on spending. The family vacation we had planned for the summer would have to be postponed. Dinners out would be curtailed, so would any unnecessary clothing expenditures.

"I was amazed at how they responded," he says. "They all seemed to want to help. Of the three of them, two immediately started looking for after-school jobs and once they had them, assured me I could discontinue their allowances and they'd be just fine. All became more thoughtful about spending money — at least until I found another position."

This is not an unusual situation. Very frequently children see trouble as a rallying point and close ranks behind you so they can feel a part of the new family.

• *List all the assets you can liquidate.* Sell anything you don't value — from the diamond necklace stashed underneath the stock certificates in the safe deposit box to the piano that hasn't been tuned for three years. Be certain to check with family members before selling these items, though. Especially in remarriages, spouses and children have important emotional attachments to material things. In a case where one of the parents has died and the other parent remarried, for example, the piano may be the focal point of memories that the child has about his deceased parent. In that case, the piano isn't an item you would sell.

Consider selling stocks, savings bonds, a second car, a boat — anything you can replace when you're on firmer financial ground.

• *Tap into hidden assets.* Some assets that don't spring to mind may be tapped or borrowed against. For example, look into borrowing against the value of a corporate pension or profit-sharing plan within federal limits (generally $50,000 or one half of your vested benefits, whichever is smaller).

If necessary, you can invade your Individual Retirement Account. The government does not limit the amount you can withdraw, although you'll pay income tax at current rates on any funds you remove before you reach 59½, plus a 10% penalty (unless the funds are used for a medical emergency).

Banks won't lend you money if you're in dire financial straits, but if you can negotiate a loan before you're perceived as a poor credit risk, do. Extend your overdraft checking privileges at the bank and increase the limit on your credit cards. (If you've been a reliable customer up until this point, banks and credit card issuers do this without asking questions.)

• *Investigate benefit options.* If you or your spouse have

been laid off or have a medical disability, ask the employer's benefits officer about the availability of payments from the corporate, federal, state, and local funds. Keep in mind that unemployment benefits are fully taxable.

If you lose your job and have vested pension benefits, you could take the money out of the plan now (rather than roll it over to an IRA or a new pension plan). If you do, you'll pay current taxes on the distribution plus a 10% penalty tax for early withdrawal. (If you need the money, you need it.) No penalty tax is imposed if the money is withdrawn as a result of death, disability, or severe medical problems, or if you're 59½ or older.

A Chance to Grow

Being pummeled by the anxiety of tense times hurts. But those husbands and wives who supported each other through the financial beatings say that, though they could have done without them, the relationship is stronger for the experience. Without exception, when the spouses reflected on the past woes, they wound up with renewed respect for one another.

Chris, 43, the only one of three siblings in the family business, had been assured by his father that he would receive sufficient equity in the business to ensure a smooth succession when the father retired. Chris relayed that assurance to Marie during their two-and-a-half-year courtship — although he was somewhat concerned that no concrete actions or plans were made to back up the promise. About the time he proposed to Marie, his father died. The bulk of the business and the building housing it were left to his mother. Chris had the mere 10% ownership stake he had been given when his father was alive. He offered to buy his mother out. Even though he had increased sales ten times since his father's semiretirement, and even though his mother had played no part in the business when her husband was alive, his mother was intransigent about relinquishing ownership and control.

Marie operates a small management consulting firm which she had painstakingly nurtured over the four and a half years since her divorce. She had been looking forward to being a wife and mother again — even to having another child — and to devoting more time to her creative side — composing music. "Money symbolizes security to me," *she explains,* "though I never have chosen a man or followed a career path because of it.*

"I would have liked the issue of ownership settled before our wedding," *Marie says,* "but since that didn't seem likely, I reasoned there was no mythical optimum time to get married. We loved each other. We'd get married as planned in July 1988.*

"I sent the invitations out. About a week later, without discussing it with me, Chris resigned from the company."

"I had taken two days off to get ready for the wedding," *Chris explains.* "The people in the office were quite competent to run it without my being there. When I got back, there were four messages that my mother had called. I returned her calls and she started berating me for my absence. I told her that if she thought she could run the business better, perhaps this would be a good time for her to try. I sent her what I thought was a reasoned letter of resignation — which was accepted without comment — and I left the business two weeks later."*

Chris opened a small export business with clients he had developed over the years. "Exporting was a side business for my mother's company and there was no one there who knew the clients or anything about the subject but me," *he says.* "I didn't raid her company for any domestic customers. I could have, but I didn't think it was the honorable thing to do."*

For about nine months, Chris's business did well. Chris's mother liquidated her company at about the same time Chris's orders started to slip — though there was no connection between the two.

Struggling to keep his business alive long enough for a big deal to come through, Chris borrowed money from the bank using the house he owned with his former wife as collateral. She agreed to sign for a home equity loan with him as long as he paid it off. But business proceeded to get worse. Since the business provided him with no income, he stopped paying alimony/support. He got sick and was hospitalized for a while. Then, not able to keep it afloat any longer, Chris closed the business and started looking for a job.

For more than a year Marie took on the financial responsibility for their life together. ''I was angry because I was draining my business of capital. I was angry because I never had threatening creditors calling the house before. I was angry because though I consider myself a liberated woman, I hadn't expected this to be a one-sided deal,'' Marie admits.

''And I panicked. Although Chris was doing everything he could to find a job, I kept thinking, 'Let him drive a cab. Let him do something.' ''

Marie didn't want the anger and panic to destroy her deep love and affection for Chris, especially because she was sympathetic to his position. She sought the help of a behavioral therapist, who pointed out that the reason Chris wasn't contributing to the family's finances was because he didn't have to. ''I was keeping everything on an even keel,'' Marie says. ''The therapist asked me what I thought would be a fair contribution for me to make to the family. I said I thought it was fair to take care of the mortgage, food, and the upkeep of the house, but that any discretionary expenditures — the housekeeper, entertainment, new clothes — should be Chris's responsibility.''

''Marie and I talked about this,'' Chris continues. ''I hated the idea of applying for unemployment benefits. But I also hated asking her for money. I realized I needed to do something, even while I was waiting for the break I was sure would come. So I went through the humbling experience of waiting on an unemployment line.

''I felt better after this,'' Chris says. ''And it took the pressure off Marie.

''There is no doubt that our relationship started healing from *the trauma we experienced during the last 18 months when Chris started to contribute to it financially,'' Marie says.*

Chris's optimism and persistence paid off. He now has a well-paying managerial position which allows him to flex his entrepreneurial muscle. There's almost a palpable sigh of relief from both of them when they talk about the next few years. Chris's debt of over $100,000 must be repaid and that will drain him of most of his income over the next three years. But then, he'll be able to lend meaningful financial support to this remarriage. Marie and Chris acknowledge they still have problems, but they have come through a major financial crisis intact and still are committed to each other. ''I feel proud of us for that,'' Marie says.

Defusing Anger

When money pressures become too great, there are practical steps you can take to defuse the resentment and safeguard your finances.

Air your feelings. Use the talk techniques in Chapter 2. Forget the legalities for a moment. Talk about how much financial responsibility you *feel* you should have for your marriage or your spouse's obligations from a former marriage and why you *feel* infuriated by using your funds to pay off the credit card debts of your spouse's children or tuition for your stepchild's private school. "When Aaron was out of work, I had a full-time managerial job and was writing a book," Sylvia said. "Resentment overwhelmed me. I told him I just couldn't keep pouring funds into his children's education. While I love those kids, I do feel they're his charges, not mine. I needed to have some money that I could assign to my own personal goals. Aaron agreed that we needed to find a fairer solution."

Don't write checks for obligations that aren't yours. Even if you wind up paying for them anyway, have your spouse write the check for his or her obligations from your joint account. Or give your check to your spouse for his or her personal account. Either way, your spouse will have the responsibility to pay the obligation personally. Aaron satisfied Sylvia's need to disassociate herself from providing money for his children by taking out a small home equity loan. "Aaron put the money in his account, and I never involved myself with his children's finances again," Sylvia said. "We reached a verbal agreement that he would repay the loan when he was working again. I can't tell you what a difference that made in how I felt."

Be empathetic . . . and as financially supportive as possible. Losing a business or losing a job is a blow to everyone, but it's most severe to the person to whom it's happening. Katie admits she didn't understand the anguish her husband must have felt from losing the business and not being able to provide support for his children until she experienced a similar incident in her life. "When I saw my husband take over all our expenses, including those relating to my three boys, I realized how meaningful sharing financial responsibilities was in a relationship."

Use the rough times to enhance rather than destroy your relationship. Success during these times depends on the depth of your commitment to each other. It also depends on a daily dash of fun and creativity. Make room during the glum times for romantic walks, relaxing massages, dancing in your carpeted living room late at night. Use the expected times of dotage — birthdays, anniversaries, and Christmas or Hanukkah — to give a gift of love your spouse will never forget. Years later, we all fondly remember and proudly use the button box, paperweight, or napkin holder our children made us. If the "make me something" approach works so well with children who have no spending money, why shouldn't it work as well with adults — on a more sophisticated level. Let me share with you a few of the most wonderful gifts I and others have ever given or received.

- To my husband, a crossword puzzle enthusiast, his own personal crossword puzzle that I developed using clues that only the two of us would know.
- To me, a month of Saturdays from my husband, to be used for me to do anything I wanted (or nothing at all), when he would cheerfully take over all the household chores from shopping to carpooling, cleaning to cooking.
- To each other because both of them had always wanted middle names, Adele and Milton exchanged initials. He became Milton A. and she became Adele M. On their anniversary they signed the papers that altered their legal names.

I wouldn't want to romanticize the times of trouble, for they're difficult and consuming. They *can* destroy relationships. But they can also solidify them. "If we could get through those early years, we can get through anything," my husband reminds me.

Chapter 7

The "Ours" Child

DID YOU KNOW . . .
- Over half of remarried couples will have a child — the "ours" child.
- Most of the "ours" children are born within two years of a remarriage.
- About one quarter of preschool stepchildren gain a half sibling in the first 18 months following remarriage.
- Of the stepchildren who are between the ages of 10 and 13 at the time of a remarriage, 16% will have a half sibling.

Maybe it's been a while since you've brought a new baby into this world. Maybe the experience is a first.

In either case, a bird's-eye view of the costs might be an eye-opener.

Figure $5,800 for the first year. At least that's what it was for a baby born in 1989, according to *American Demographics* magazine. Today, just to seat babies, we have body slings, car seats, infant seats, restaurant seats, high chairs, umbrella strollers — and a whole array of double-duty contraptions. Since more than 56% of mothers with children under the age of six work, day-care expenses are included in the first year's costs. They're substantial.

All precious things increase in value. Babies are precious. So we can expect their costs to continue to increase.

A family with average earnings of $50,000 will spend over $260,000 to feed, clothe, and shelter little Sally until she's 22. That's just the beginning. If you want to send her to private or parochial school, give her piano, tennis, skiing, or karate lessons, or help with her college tuition, magnify the basic figure once, twice, three times. There are other financial realities to contend with.

- Other children in the family may also depend on us for economic security.
- The cost of higher education has outpaced inflation — and probably will continue to do so.
- The real estate market won't be what it was in the 1980s — an almost instant way to build equity. Now, the fact that our homes appreciate at a slower, saner rate means we will have less equity to tap into.
- Because we may be having this child at a later time in our lives, there's a good chance her college years will butt up against our retirement years — doubling the pressure of "low income–high expense" times.

All that said, children are blessings, not assets. They can't be evaluated by formulas or by financial worth. And in a remarriage, there is considerable evidence that the "ours" child can enrich the stepfamily. In the conclusion of her book *Yours, Mine, and Ours: How Families Change When Remarried Parents Have a Child Together,* Anne Bernstein talks about her own experience and those of the people she spoke to. "What emerges from the variety and complexity of the interviews is a portrait of stepfamily life that, while not without blemish, becomes more dimensional and vibrant when it includes at least 'one that's ours.' "

A Meeting of the Minds

Getting married might be the easiest decision you ever made; deciding to have an "ours" child might be the most difficult. Not everyone who remarries wants one. I did — even though I had three and my husband had five. My husband didn't. When the reality and enormity of our joint responsibilities touched every dollar and emotion we had, which happened within the first month of marriage, I changed my mind. Eight *was* enough. Best to right what's left, I decided hurriedly, than bring in and bring up another.

Other people come to different conclusions. To a large degree, the number of children a woman has had before remarriage will influence the decision on whether to have another. Understandably, women with two or more children already are, statistically, significantly less likely to give birth in the second marriage. So, too, with men. But since most men choose to remarry women who are younger than their first wives, it is more likely that the partner without children will be the woman.

The decision to have or not have an "ours" child often becomes part of the marriage negotiations, says psychologist Bernstein. It was with Stuart, who has three children from a former marriage, and Carole, who has no children and has never been married before.

"At first Stuart said 'yes'; he wanted more children," Carole says. *"And that was important to me. I came from a large, loving family and wanted at least one of my own."*

As his children became a heavier and heavier financial drain, Stuart changed his mind. "It was a difficult time in our marriage," Carole recalls. *"His unilateral decision prompted a sense of desolation in me. I was so depressed, I went to see a therapist. With her help, I was able to articulate my desires and my needs to him."*

Says Stuart, "Our relationship had gotten to the point that we were going in opposite directions. I didn't want that. One Sunday

I went to church — something I hadn't done for years. Strangely, and I do mean strangely because I'm not a religious person, I had a vision of a bird coming down and putting his wings around me and saying that everything would be all right. I took that as a sign that if we had a child together, we would be able to handle it."

They now have one daughter and one son, ages three and one. Carole works part-time as a physical therapist in a Boston suburb. Stuart has a solid managerial position and earns enough to cover the additional expenses.

"If any decision was made based on an act of faith," Stuart says with a laugh, "having our children was."

Ages and numbers of other children in the family, ages of husband and wife, attitudes of both partners about parent-hood, where each partner is in the life cycle, how strongly one of the partners wants a child — all these are considerations when making a decision on having a child of your own.

So, too, are the financial considerations, such as how you will replace the loss of income if one parent, presumably the wife, stays home with the new baby or works part-time. Jancey and Ralph have a problem. They (but most vocifer-ously, she) would like to have a child together. She would like to "play mom" and stay home with this child, some-thing she wasn't able to do with her son from a prior mar-riage. But Ralph's small advertising agency is on the verge of bankruptcy. Without the substantial income from her one-woman personnel agency, they couldn't live. "Since Ralph is not able to be the sole support of the family now, I'd rather wait to have the child — even though, at 41, I don't have much time."

Steps to Take Before or When "Ours" Arrives

Beef up your emergency fund. When baby no longer makes three — more like four or five or six or seven — there can rarely be too much money in an emergency fund: money you can draw on at a moment's notice. The rule of thumb is to have three months' worth of living expenses readily available for an emergency. Since a woman frequently takes anywhere from three weeks to six months off from paid employment after giving birth, fortify your money market fund or account reserves to cover at least four months' worth of expenses. If you don't have the funds to transfer, stash the savings from a reduction in spending or from a cutback in contributions to other accounts, such as IRAs or retirement plans like 401(k)s.

Update and increase your insurance. If you're an income producer, your income probably is needed to maintain the family's standard of living. The odds are far greater that you'll suffer a disability that will keep you away from work for more than three months than they are that you will die. Do you have adequate long-term disability coverage to handle this possibility?

And life insurance. If your other children are beneficiaries of the policy, do you want to add this child as well? If your spouse is the beneficiary, do you want to increase the coverage so he or she will have more resources to cover this child's expenses in the event of your death?

Too, add this baby to your health coverage. You have 30 days from the date of birth to do it without proving medical insurability.

Claim an extra withholding allowance. Because you'll be claiming an additional dependency exemption on your tax return, you'll be paying less in taxes (assuming a level income). By changing your W-4 form (which determines how much tax is withheld from your paycheck), you'll be boosting your take-home pay.

Start an education fund. Gift money from relatives can be used to seed a college fund. You can buy U.S. Series EE Savings bonds, which accumulate interest tax-free while you own them. If you cash them in during a year that you pay college tuition for the child, you might not pay tax on the accumulated interest. There's a total exemption from taxes for couples whose adjusted gross income isn't more than $60,000. It phases out until your adjusted gross income reaches $90,000. Then you lose the exemption entirely.

You might also consider buying tax-exempt bond funds or growth-oriented mutual funds that are earmarked for your child's education. These let you keep control of the money and, in the case of a tax-exempt fund, give you a tax break as well.

If you put the assets in your child's name, you do so with a custodial account. The tax savings in transferring money to children have been reduced somewhat over the past years, but still they exist. Until your child reaches age 14, the first $500 of her investment income is tax-free, the next $500 is taxed at the child's rate (almost always a better rate than yours), and any additional earnings are taxed at your rate.

Revise your estate plan. How you plan to take care of this child in case of your death depends upon how much money is available and whether or not this is your only natural child. Says an Atlanta estate attorney, "If this is a woman's first child, often she will fight and scream if her husband doesn't provide for this child better than he is for his children from a former marriage."

You will want to reexamine your wills. First, you have to name a guardian for this child, in the event that both of you die. This can be a problem. If there are other children living in your family, presumably they will be cared for by your former spouse. That means your child will be shuttled off to a relative or friend while her half siblings (to whom she might be very close) will go in another direction. Unless yours is an unusual setup, siblings will be split.

For the parent whose only child is "ours," there are fewer questions about who, eventually, will be the heir. More estate planning challenges face the parent who has two or more sets of children.

There are a variety of solutions. Here are three.

Donna and Roy have two children together and Roy has three from a former marriage who live with their mother. "We split things among the kids to reflect the fact that if we both die, two out of five children would have lost both parents and three of the five would have lost one," says Donna. "Roy and I split our property. One half is mine; one half his. My will gives my property to our two children. His is divided up five ways because he has five children. We each have life insurance naming each other as beneficiary. This arrangement feels fair to both of us."

Antoinette has two sons, one from a former marriage and one with her husband Owen. She has left her whole estate in trust for both children. For as long as he's alive, Owen has the right to all the interest from the trust and can even invade principal if he needs it. On his death, the estate will be divided by both Antoinette's children. Owen's plan is different. At the time of his death, half his estate will go to Antoinette directly and the other half will go into a trust that would benefit her during her lifetime but upon her death would go to their son.

Leslie and Edward have two daughters together. Edward also has a son from a previous marriage. "My son lives with his mother, who has inherited over a million dollars from her father, and his stepfather, a nice chap who is wealthy in his own right," says Edward. "I know my son will be well cared for by his mother, so I'm not going to worry about his sharing in my estate. That will go to my wife and daughters. But I don't want him to feel I'm leaving him nothing, so I've taken out an insurance policy — which names him as the beneficiary and leaves him a token amount of money."

How do you divide your estate among children in their

teens or 20s and a young child? "A young child must be thought of in a different context," affirms New York matrimonial attorney Jacalyn Barnett. "He or she needs more than an 18-year-old who already has been supplied with many things. So though leaving unequal amounts to different children may appear unfair if the numbers are placed alongside each other, I don't think it necessarily is." A trust that allows the trustee to distribute or sprinkle funds to children where and when they are needed, such as for the care and education of the younger children, can be established to handle the looming needs of the younger children. Eventually, when the younger children are grown, whatever is left of the legacy can be divided among all the children.

Because teen or adult children can interpret the inequality of the bequests as an inequality of love, you do best to explain the rationale of your decisions to those children old enough to understand and those who might feel slighted by the apportionment. Remember, too, that money isn't everything. More precious to many are the heirlooms and family mementos, which should be given or bequested to those for whom they would have most meaning.

How "Ours" Affects Family Finances

Unless you're able to increase the size of the financial pie, or the pie is unusually large, having another child will affect the resources available to other children in the family. There might be less for "his" and "hers." But that's part of any family situation. More financial responsibility means more sharing.

Parents have to stay alert to the fact that teenagers sometimes see the little intruder as putting a hand directly in their pockets, even when that's not the case. "I thought my mother and stepfather would ante up for a car this year because most of my friends' parents did. But then the baby came and they said 'no,' " Robert recounts. It took a score of

hours of arguing and then explaining for Robert to understand that the turndown wasn't linked to the baby. "They
don't think a 16-year-old should have a car of his own,"
Robert says. "They have said that if I decide I want a car in
two years and work to save the money for it, they'll provide
me with matching funds. I'm surprised and a bit annoyed
because I assumed something so different. But I have to
admit they're not mean. We just never talked about this
before." The excitement of a pregnancy and the chaos of
establishing a family life worked against solid communication. Robert's parents never found out what Robert was
thinking and he assumed they knew.

Having a baby together blurs the financial separateness of
most remarriages. Not that husbands and wives are going to
abandon their individual accounts. They probably won't. But
the joint account that was slim or never established before
the birth of their baby will swell. "Ours" children are cradled
in "our" money.

And that commitment to joint spending and joint funds
spills over into the whole extended family. "It wasn't until
our daughter was born that I began to understand why Jack
was so generous to his children," Eleanor says. "Even though
I still catch myself in a 'why-is-he-buying-them-the-best-
sled-for-Christmas-not-the-least-expensive' mode once in a
while, now, for the most part, I can appreciate why he spends
what he does. In fact, I'm the one who urges that we buy his
children more now."

Though there are no hard statistics to bear this out, ob-
servers conclude that in many instances "ours" children provide the stepchildren with a rallying point and give weight to
the remarried couple's commitment to an enduring relationship.

Chapter 8

Financial Links
To Former Spouses, Stepchildren . . . and Beyond

DID YOU KNOW . . .

- Divorced women are more likely than widows to remarry, so there are usually former husbands in the remarriage picture.
- Women with children are more likely than women without children to remarry, so their children have two father figures — a biological father and a stepfather.
- A custodial mother who remarries has more frequent contact with former in-laws than one who doesn't.
- Changes in custody arrangements are common at the time of a remarriage.
- The quality of the stepparent-stepchild relationship is the best predictor of how a stepchild will grow into adulthood.
- Stepparent's Day is celebrated on the first Sunday of October in nine states.

Remarriage is its own special entity. It can't be, shouldn't be, and doesn't work if it tries to be a facsimile of a first marriage. When you remarry, you create a real family, but it's unique because of its complexity and because the financial links often are as extended as the number of people you are or *were* related to. For every complicated financial arrangement with a member of the extended family, a myriad of creative solutions exist. To uncover them you have to come to terms with a new reality, invent tradition, and unrein your imagination.

In the best of all possible worlds, you and your present family would have enough money to live comfortably; your former spouses and children not living with you would have the same. No jealousy or vindictiveness would mar the general well-being and spirit of cooperation of all the loosely linked families. But that's rarely the case. Some children wind up with more; some with less. Some families barely scrape by; some prosper.

Former family members stay financially linked for many years and through many subsequent marriages. Many will agree with Paul, who says that's "too long." "Because we never had children and I have remarried, I thought we'd never have anything to do with one another again," he says of his first wife. "That's not the way it is, though. Her attorney calls mine once a year — like clockwork — seeking more alimony." And when there are children from a former marriage, the financial ties string out over years. The remarried challenge is to fulfill financial obligations to former families at the same time you build a financial base with your new family. If the ideas offered here don't fit your situation, build on them to create your own solutions.

Financial Links with Former Spouses

Alimony. When the vitriol between former spouses still surges, writing an alimony check can be stressful. The deed must be done; no debate about that. But how? One man whose former wife had an account at the same bank he did simply made an arrangement with the bank to transfer funds automatically from his account to hers each month. This can often be arranged even if former spouses have accounts at different banks.

Another option: If your new spouse doesn't have the same enmity, ask her to write the check. If it's from a joint account and she signs it, make certain it's marked "January alimony from Sam Smith." If she fills in the check from your account, you'll need to sign it. But perhaps if it's tucked in among other checks requiring your signature it won't evoke strong passion. Don't be surprised if a residual of rancor seeps in when the second wife makes out the alimony check, however. Says Alaine, "I write it out and it's always on time. But my little noogie is to put the return address sticker on the envelope, which has my name, not Peter's."

The most positive approach and a good long-range solution to the alimony angst is to talk yourself into another frame of mind when you're writing the check. Instead of focusing on the money that your "rotten, conniving" former spouse is getting, interpret the act of writing the check as evidence of what a responsible and caring person you are.

Court actions. Nothing prevents a former spouse from suing for more money for support or to enforce some unimportant violation in a separation agreement (such as your not sending, annually, a copy of a life insurance policy with he or she named as beneficiary). Nor is anything more shattering to a remarriage than a former spouse's intrusion by subpoena. Pile the emotional damage onto the financial — having to pay lawyers megabucks to defend yourself on frivolous charges — and you have a nasty situation. Some courts, clogged with more important family matters, have no patience or time for what they consider nuisance suits and, after a number of such, stipulate there will be sanctions assessed against the party losing the suit. Often the sanctions include paying for the winning party's attorney's fees (in addition to one's own attorney) and all court costs. In an effort to discourage lawyers from taking these suits, some courts also order the losing attorney to pay a penalty.

Stepparents are not legally required to support stepchildren under most circumstances. So, for example, if a former wife is suing for more support, and to justify her claim she states that you can afford to pay more because of what your new wife earns, she's probably not going to get far. Even if she sees a joint tax return filed by you and your spouse, the stepparent's income is rarely used to calculate support.

Money messengers. Don't saddle children with relaying money messages to a former spouse, and don't allow your former spouse to do it either. When a child comes to you relaying a request for more money for his or her custodial parent, don't get sucked into discussing it. Tell the child that you're providing the other parent with the funds you had agreed to and that any additional money discussions are between you and the other parent. You're relieving the child of the onerous burden of acting as a go-between — a position children should never be in. As for whether to meet the requests for additional support, that's a decision you have to make. If you can afford it and the request seems reasonable, then you might choose to do so. If you can't, you might refuse.

Financial decisions concerning children. The person who pays the bills has more influence over decisions. That may not be fair, but it's reality. But what do you do when both biological parents contribute to the children's support and feel keenly about their welfare but are at loggerheads about some monetary decision? For example, what if you don't agree on whether your child should go to private school? Or what if, even though you both subscribe to that concept, you can't agree on which one?

To move beyond the sparks-flying stage, consider working with a third party — someone trained in techniques of family mediation. In a bit of a twist, one that can be successful only if there is an amicable relationship between the nuclear and the stepfamilies, Natalie, the stepmother, serves as a mediator. "I think it works because both parents and the children see me as the objective third party — and because both parents honestly try to make decisions that are in the best interest of their children. And," she admits, "it certainly helps that I have no children of my own, and that we have enough money so that no one feels deprived."

Keep in mind that solutions to problems take negotiation, compromise, persistence, and time.

You can't pay what you owe to a former spouse. It happens. Even when you have the best of intentions, a business fails, a family member needs money for a serious medical problem, the value of investments set aside for children's education evaporates — and the funds that had been promised are not available as planned. You have four choices.

1. Assuming your former spouse is amenable, you can work with each other or through a third party to mediate a resolution. Rodney, who has a separation agreement that calls for half the tuition of a state college to be borne by each parent, didn't have the money when his daughter was ready for school. "So my former wife and I agreed that she'd pay it," he explains, "and when she sells the house she and my children are living in, she will take the tuition money out of my share."

Joyce, another financially squeezed parent who was unable to ante up the college funds she thought she'd have by the time her son was ready for college, made a verbal commitment to him and to his custodial father. He was to apply for financial aid. When he graduated, she would help him pay back the loan. That proved to be an acceptable arrangement.

2. You can look for the needed money elsewhere, assuming it's available: parents, relatives, banks, or new spouse. As a loan, this approach works only if there is a reasonable prospect you'll be able to repay it and the loan sources sub-

scribe to the deal — financially and emotionally. One new spouse was delighted to come to the assistance of her husband, whose business was in a slump. "As long as I have the extra money," she says, "I have no problem using it toward my stepson's tuition." In that case the money was a gift.

3. You can risk getting sued (if you're the debtor) or you can institute suit (if you're the person to whom money is owed).

4. You can resign yourself to not getting the money. Or, if you're the one reneging, resign yourself to the consequences of being delinquent, which often includes the wrath of children as well as a former spouse.

Children as ragamuffins. You provide your former spouse with what you consider a sizable support check each month, yet when the children come visiting each summer, they're in tatters. You and your spouse wind up buying them everything from toothbrushes to swimsuits. And it galls you. Forget the fleeting thought that you'll subtract the amount spent from the next support check. That's not on the up-and-up. Those items that might be reused each visit — toothbrush, comb, beach towels, robes, and oversize sweatshirts — can be kept at your home for future stays. Those items the children will outgrow from visit to visit should be packed in their suitcases when they return home.

Children's weddings. The guiding rule during these high-stress times, according to stepfamily experts John and Emily Visher, is that everyone concerned should concentrate at this time on how the young person would like this affair to go and not on "evening the score" or resolving old issues between households. Those precepts hold no matter who pays for what.

Unless the young person has no relationship with his or her other biological parent, the nonpaying parent and his or her spouse should be invited, as well as the young person's close relatives on that side of the family. Beyond that, there are personal choices. Is the invited parent asked to contribute for his or her invites? Does the nonpaying parent play a dominant role in the wedding planning and ceremony? Who pays for the prenuptial dinner? The wedding attire of attendants (especially if they're members of another household)?

Alternatives to traditional large weddings work well when there are problems between two households. Small weddings in the offices of a clergy person, a judge, or on board a boat (performed by an authorized ship's captain) can be memorable. Before or after the actual ceremony, families can host parties, jointly or separately, honoring the young couple.

One Family Linked to Another

Even if they are hundreds of miles apart, former families and new families *seem* to know exactly how the other is living — and it's always extravagantly. "I know they are spending thousands on renovations and going away on lavish vacations," says Marge, even though she admits these conclusions are based on bits and pieces of information provided by her five-year-old son, Kevin, after he came home from a two-week stay at his father and stepmother's house. "And we never go anywhere."

Stepmother Judy was astonished when she learned of what Marge was saying. "We're always scrimping. Marge and her husband are the wealthy ones. They have two cars — one a Mercedes. And they went on a lovely holiday while Kevin was visiting us."

Whatever side of the financial line you're on, it seems like the wrong side.

This is true especially with children, who because of their lack of sophistication and their confusion over the remarriage configuration, often assume that the kids living in the "other" house are getting more.

Telling children about the family's finances. For those remarrieds who are bringing into the fold children from a former marriage, there is always the question of what children should be told about the couple's new financial picture. That's true in biologically intact families too, but in remarriages the questions are complicated because the issues are more complex and there are more people involved. Also, most remarrieds aren't anxious to give children information about their finances that the children will later share with a former spouse.

Much of the decision about what to tell and what not to tell, of course, depends on the age and maturity of the children as well as how comfortable the adults (all of them — parents and stepparents) are in discussing the situation.

Given the swirling changes that remarriage brings to children, parents have to try to keep money and financial problems from creating more stress for them. Money talks can become a vehicle to further unity, if by words and deed they can assure the child of the couple's commitment to each other and to each other's children. Without drawing children into the fray with former spouses, parents and stepparents have to be able to explain problems as unemotionally as possible in ways that do not make the children feel they are the cause of the plight or responsible for finding the solutions to financial problems. In some cases where the children are old enough to understand, it makes sense to explain, where they're involved, the terms of a separation agreement signed with a former spouse.

"My kids were pissed off at me because their mother told them she wasn't getting alimony," Barney relays. "What she didn't tell them was the reason for that. I've had a heart condition for many years. When we were divorced, we decided she should have the house and 90% of our savings, because I can't be assured of how long I'll be working. This way she and the children wouldn't have to count on my being healthy for their daily bread. When they understood the reasons behind the agreement, our relationship improved and they didn't think I was stiffing them anymore."

Phone calls. Rarely does the phone bill between former spouses become excessive. They are usually all too happy to keep their conversations brief.

It's those long-distance calls made by your children or stepchildren to their noncustodial parent that are astronomical. You suspect the children are pouring out their unhappiness with your new marriage, and you're steamed that you have to pay for it.

No matter how well it seems to be going, remarriage is difficult and confusing for children. They face divided loyalties and resent any attempt you make to limit contact with the noncustodial parent. On the other hand, you can't give them free rein to run up phone bills.

You have a number of options or combinations of options.

• Make certain you are on the long-distance service that best suits this particular situation. All the major companies have their own supersaver programs designed for people who spend more than $8 a month on long-distance calls: AT&T's is Reach Out America; MCI's is Prime Time; Sprint's Sprint Plus.

• Ask children to restrict their calls to low-rate hours. Sunday evening isn't one of them. But all day Saturday is; so is Sunday until 5:00 P.M. and any evening (usually after 5:00 P.M. on the supersaver programs).

• Set limits on the length of calls to the parent, but make the limits realistic. If the children need to talk beyond that, ask them to have the parent call back.

• If the children are teens — which, by definition, means the phone is a problem — consider installing a separate phone line for them. You can tell them you'll pay up to a given dollar amount each month and they're responsible for the rest. Or, as long as they're able to earn their own money, they can be asked to pay the entire monthly tab. Teens like the privacy of their own lines. Having them contribute to the bill is a valuable money management lesson.

Kids play the fairness issue. Get used to it. Until children are old enough and have had enough distance from the emotional upheavals of divorce and remarriage to assess the situation objectively, the grass on the other family's lawn will not only be greener, it will be more expensive as well. They will see inequities — real or not — and, often without realizing what they are doing, will play on the initial confusion (and perhaps guilt) associated with the remarriage to put the squeeze on parents for a new toy, bike, or car. And parents are easy targets — especially Disneyland Dads, those fathers whose children are treated to whirlwind entertainment when they visit. These fathers (in some cases mothers) feel guilty or badly about not being a full-time presence in their children's lives, so they try to make up for it with things and amusements. Especially when money is tight, this extraordinary treatment rankles other members of the new family. Expensive entertainment, writes Marcella Sabo in *Whose Kid Is It Anyway?*, "could certainly create worry for a wife and cause her to feel a sense of inadequacy regarding what she can provide for her own children." The option: more talk, games, and at-home activities that allow for a natural interaction between parent and visiting child.

We as parents shouldn't get caught in the "she got something I didn't get" competition that children are especially adept at playing — whether they're stepsiblings or siblings of a nuclear family. They want us to equate fairness with equality, which, of course, is not accurate. In actuality, equality warps fairness. Would it be fair to give your six-year-old son and 12-year-old stepson the same allowance? Or deprive a musically gifted child of violin lessons simply because her stepsiblings aren't talented? Would you go out on an equal financial limb to support two children in college — one who pulls all-nighters in the library and the other in pubs? "Being relentlessly equal negates the connection between money and need, which is the real issue when it comes to financial fairness," says Claire Berman, author of *Making It As a Stepfamily.*

While a grand display of unequal gift giving is inappropriate, the value of a present should not, of course, be measured by how much is spent on it. The best way to give a gift is to concentrate on its meaning, not its cost. A compact disc component to a music enthusiast, an outfit to a clotheshorse, or a special toy for a toddler may not be equal in price, but in the eyes of the receiver each is special and valued.

Kids are masters at pressuring or manipulating parents with the "You're not fair" taunt. When they're in their teens, nettlesome sullenness or freshness replaces the childish challenge. Instead of caving in to some perceived guilt, we as adults have to be clear about what we can spend and then explain it to our children.

Josh and Ginny admit they've spent many an evening holed up on their bed grappling with the fact that one child, his, is going to private college and the other, hers, will not. "But we finally got together on it," Ginny says, "and are presenting a united front: Going to a private college isn't an inalienable right." Says Josh: "My stepdaughter, Laura, drives a used BMW that Ginny and I bought for her when she turned 16. Now she's 18 and wants to go to the University of Pennsylvania like my son did. But that was six years ago and college costs have risen dramatically — more than our income, I might add. We can afford the tuition for the state university, but my feeling is that if Laura wants to go to Penn, she should contribute something — perhaps by selling her car and using that money. She now accuses us of being unfair. 'What has my car got to do with going to Penn?' she asks. Thank heavens Ginny and I talked this out beforehand, because I really care for Laura and don't want to come out the heavy on this issue by leading Ginny or Laura to believe I'm playing favorites."

"Sure I want to help all our children with their college educations," says Joe, a Detroit-based computer sales representative. "And they know that. But I've also told them that while my son didn't have to work while he was in school because his grandparents covered most of the costs, Julie's girls, my stepdaughters, will. They don't have the same financial reservoir. They'll get some money from us, but not enough to cover all their expenses. You could say that's not fair — especially since at least one of the girls is a better student than my son. But life isn't always fair. Nor is fairness the issue here. This is a monetary decision."

The fact that one set of biological grandparents are wealthy and eager to assume some responsibility for their grandchild's education further emphasizes the unevenness of the playing field — not unusual in remarriages. Husband and wife come to the new marriage with varying assets — some personal, some familial. They've had more time and opportunity to build both assets and debts than they had in a first marriage. So have their families. And if there is a noncustodial parent providing additional support, that's another imbalance.

Among the most important factors in determining who gets what among stepsiblings are the ages and needs of the children. Resources will be mobilized for a 10-year-old with a serious medical problem that will not be available to the 18-year-old who would like a car, for example. And anyone who has reared children knows that a teenager's financial needs outstrip a toddler's.

Differing attitudes. In remarriages, spouses often bring very disparate values involving money to the marriage. As a matter of principle, William feels children should be responsible for their own college education. His wife, Elsie, on the other hand, thinks it's her duty to make certain her children's every educational need is met, and she's willing to work two jobs to assure that. So, depending on how committed William's children are to furthering their education, it may be that Elsie's children will go to college immediately after high school and William's won't.

Living with imbalance. Laurie and Michael have the classic stepfamily inequity situation — one they have very little control over. Laurie explains it.

"I'm in my second year of a three-year master's degree program in social work so I'm not earning anything now. My husband, Michael, is a drug rehabilitation counselor at a clinic. His salary plus interest from an inheritance from his mother are just enough to support us and our baby daughter. My former husband, Patrick, and I have joint custody of our two teenage boys, which means the boys are with Michael and me four days a week and with Patrick for three. Although Patrick pays for the boys' clothes and allowances, we cover whatever it costs for them when they're with us — food, school lunch money, and the like. By separation agreement, I'm also expected to contribute a monthly sum to a fund which takes care of the boys' educational and recreational expenses — but I have been unable to do that since I gave birth. The problem is that Patrick, who is a major executive with a large drug firm, makes more than he can spend and has no other financial responsibilities. So there is a real difference in what the boys can do and get in the two households." Laurie says that though the children have adjusted to some of the restrictions imposed by her current economic situation, they continue to press for certain amenities, like unlimited telephone use, which they enjoy at one home and not the other.

"I find myself caught between the desire to please the boys and the need to pay attention to economic realities," she says. *"And don't think the boys don't occasionally try to exploit my guilt at having wanted the divorce and putting them in this situation in the first place."*

The issue is further tested because Michael is pressing Laurie to *sue Patrick for child support. ''Even if it was $50 a week it would help with our grocery bills,'' Michael says. ''It's only fair if he wants the boys to be happy.'' Laurie is unwilling to petition the court at the moment.*

There's no doubt that there's a considerable financial disparity between Laurie and Michael's household and Patrick's. The question, however, is Is it unfair? And if it is, to whom? To Laurie? To Michael? To the boys?

Unless the deprivation at Laurie and Michael's is extreme and the boys are starving when they're there (which Laurie assured me wasn't the case), fairness isn't the paramount issue. Laurie and Michael have to explain to the boys, in as much detail as possible, how the two households differ — excising from the discussion and the tone of their voices the resentment and anger they now feel. The subtle life lessons that money isn't everything, that fairness doesn't equal sameness or happiness, eventually will be learned. In the long run, it's more important for Laurie and Michael to accept this temporary financial strain than to worry about parity between the households or feel guilty that it doesn't exist.

The reality is that money does tie two households together. Unless both households operate independently of each other financially, any disparity between former spouses can become a thorny issue or a way to bully decisions in favor of the monied parent. Disparity not only affects the former spouses, it drags in new spouses as well. Indeed, writes Patricia Lowe in *The Cruel Stepmother*, ''Unless all concerned have plenty of money, it may and probably will influence the climate between the divorced parents and their offspring through the growing-up period. It touches decisions about education, housing, clothing, vacations, the medical and dental services chosen, and a whole raft of other problems sticky enough in their own right.''

Financial strains as a result of money paid to a former

household can have a dramatic influence on a remarriage, especially in the early years.

Andrea and Joe have been married for four years. She chronicles their life, first as it was molded by Joe's financial commitment to his first family, and later as they began to shape it together. "I spent the first year of marriage brooding about how unfair it was that we had to wait to have a child because Joe was committed to finish paying for his children's college education and felt we couldn't afford to do both. After all, I was 36 and concerned about the proverbial biological clock. Then I asked myself if the tradeoff was worth it. Was being married to Joe important enough for me to move beyond the pale of what's fair? Even before the birth of our child last year, I determined it was." Andrea has developed a philosophy over the years that has worked well for her. "Life is made up of choices. I knew Joe and I would have some difficult financial times, that his former wife would probably live more affluently than I would, but I chose to marry someone I loved. That's that."

Links Between Stepparents and Stepchildren

Stepparents often have strong emotional bonds to their stepchildren. So despite what the law says about their financial obligations, they often are eager to help with part or all of the children's financial support — as if they were the biological parent.

Legal responsibility for children. The law differs from state to state, but generally, as a stepparent, you are not legally responsible for children who don't live with you.

What about those who do?

Primary financial responsibility lies with the biological parents. But suppose you're the stepfather and the child's biological father has disappeared or died. Your wife has little or no money of her own. To avoid the possibility of the child becoming a public charge, most states hold to the position that you, the stepfather, must assume some financial responsibility.

As long as they can afford it, providing necessities doesn't bother most stepparents. The troubling aspects of financial support are more subtle. Do you ante up money for a car after your stepchild's biological parent refuses? Do you help with medical school tuition because you care about your stepchild and don't want her saddled with debt when she graduates? Do you make certain that your stepson has the same access to college funds that your own son has? These are personal questions with personal answers.

Money to stepchildren. For some children or stepchildren, asking for money is very difficult. They feel childish, humiliated, or generally uncomfortable about being on the receiving end. For others, money is an entitlement, due them simply because they are here on earth and ask for it.

''When do I say 'no' and when do I say 'yes' to requests for money?'' asks one stepmother of three teenagers, who, because she has no children of her own, has little experience in this area.

There are good reasons to say no.

- You can't afford it.
- You'd like to help out in another way. In the case of college tuition, for example, offer to work on the financial aid form with the youngster or suggest various sources for grants and scholarships.
- You think the request is irresponsible. Money for the teen's car (he's wrecked two already) is not high on your priority list.
- You don't like the youngster and he or she doesn't like you. Stepchild or not, you still have the right to refuse money to someone for personal reasons.
- You think you can buy the child's love. ''If I get the

concert tickets for her, she'll finally talk to me." No. She's not going to stop being hard as nails because you're a soft touch. Her hostility will continue, because she knows now she can get what she wants from you, civil or not.

There are good reasons to say yes.

- You can afford it.
- It's a source of personal pleasure to help out someone you care about.

Chances are the longer you and the stepchildren live together or know one another, the closer you will become and the more likely you will be to want to help out financially.

Financial aid for higher education and stepparents. Comprehensive financial aid forms ask for financial information from the parent with whom the child lived for most of the past 12 months. And, despite the fact that the stepparent has no legal financial responsibility for his stepchild, the evaluation of aid will be based on the parent and stepparent's combined incomes and assets — even if some of the assets are owned separately. It makes no sense to exclude the other biological parent's finances on this form, but that's the way it is. The information is reported to each school your child applies to.

Because colleges realize the picture painted in the comprehensive form is not always accurate (and in the case of stepfamilies rarely is), they almost always will provide their own separate financial aid applications. Here's an opportunity to tell all, including what your former spouse has agreed to pay and where he lives, and to give his home and work phone numbers — or to explain if he has skipped town.

Expensive colleges are more likely to require information and money from the other biological parent than state or public schools. Rarely, however, do they get into the collection game. If a man, for example, refuses to honor a separation agreement made with his former wife that calls for a $7,000 a year contribution toward each child's college education, it is the wife, not the college, who will have to bring suit to collect it.

But even if the father does pay, the sum will not normally reduce the contribution expected from the mother and stepfather. Sorry to say, but most colleges simply will reduce your child's aid package by the amount anteed up by the noncustodial parent. And usually the reduction comes from the "free" money portion of the package (money that doesn't have to be repaid, like grants).

Sometimes a couple is in a position to and wants to help all the children (his, hers, theirs) with college expenses. One fair way of divvying the pot is to calculate what each child will need and set up one savings (or investment) account. Each spouse contributes to the fund, even if the amounts differ substantially, and together they parcel out the money to each child based on need and the size of the account.

Legal rights of stepparents. Our legal system is bollixed up. While many stepparents provide full financial support for their stepchildren, they have few legal rights. Actually, a biological parent who deserts his or her children has greater legal rights to the children than the stepparent who rears and educates them.

Stepparents, for example, have no legal right to authorize medical treatment for their stepchildren, even though they may be acting as a parent. Until the schools and camps start devising their own forms that include spaces for names and contact information of stepparents, Richard S. Victor, Birmingham, Michigan, family law specialist, suggests the spouse who is the biological parent in the household draft several identical letters, like the one at right. Have each notarized, and keep one on file at home and at school or summer camp.

I, _____ ,
(name of biological parent)

_____ , of
(indicate whether father or mother of children)

_____
(names of children)

whose birthdays are _____ ,
(fill in dates)

hereby allow _____ to secure
(name of stepparent)

medical attention/treatment/tests on behalf of my children.

_____
(signature of biological/custodial parent)

(notary public validation)

Stepparents and their spouses must be vocal in addressing the legal issues surrounding the recognition of stepparent involvement in families so that the new family structures are acknowledged and understood.

Adoption. Like marriage, the legal rite of adoption has a subtle but profound, "connected" effect on a family. Also like marriage, it shouldn't be entered into lightly. From the stepparent's view, it's a financial obligation that extends beyond the marriage. If a couple get divorced, the adoptive stepparent is as responsible for the child's support as if he or she were the biological parent.

Because the task of adopting a stepchild whose parent is still alive is formidable, most adoptions involve stepparents who are married to widows or widowers. In instances where there is a living parent, he or she must agree to surrender all parental rights. If the noncustodial parent can't be found or if he or she refuses to concede the rights, the adoption can't be consummated.

Carefully consider the child's position before starting these proceedings. He or she might not want to be adopted, especially if adoption is proposed within a few years of the death of a biological parent. Children have problems with name changes, so you might consider using his or her present last name as a middle name and hyphenating it to the new name.

Custody rights. "Stepparent's custody" is almost an oxymoron. But there's hope. About half the fifty states have established legal rights of stepparents dealing with custody/visitation and support of minor children. Michigan matrimonial attorney Richard Victor, legal adviser for the Stepfamily Association of America, sees stepparent custody and visitation rights as "the wave of the future." Let's hope so. Stepchildren and stepparents often develop tremendous love for one another and need to have visitation guaranteed by law.

One More Link: Stepgrandparents

Unequal gift giving. You can't force grandparents to spend the same amounts on Christmas or Hanukkah presents for their stepgrandchildren as they do on their grandchildren. But you want to avoid a hurtful caste system that has the Brahmin child beaming over a stereo and the pariah brooding over a bookmark. Most grandparents, because their roles are new, are inept as stepgrandparents, not purposely mean or thoughtless. To help them, remarried couples have developed some ingenious techniques to lighten up the gift-giving occasions.

• They invent traditions, such as using a grab-bag approach to gift giving, allowing only homemade gifts during the holiday season, or giving gifts to charity instead of the family. Some families spend the holiday volunteering services at a hospital or homeless shelter.

• One woman has her children make something for their stepgrandparents. Then, a few weeks before Christmas, she casually mentions to her in-laws how long and hard the kids have been working on this "surprise" gift. Knowing how much energy went into a "special" gift softens the reluctant stepgrandparents' hearts and prompts them to reciprocate.

• Another woman talked to her in-laws about how lonely and strange her kids feel at the holidays and how they miss all the "old" faces at celebrations. The stepgrandparents understood because they, too, were feeling nostalgic for "what was." That was the bond they needed to be more thoughtful.

Stepgrandparent rights. All 50 states now have laws dealing with the issue of visitation between grandparents and grandchildren. Especially meaningful to remarrieds is one that allows a father and mother of a deceased parent to visit their grandchild even if that grandchild has been adopted by a stepparent. And that's a real plus — both for the grandparent and the child. The child now has two sets of grandparents on the "father's" side; one set doesn't replace the other. That's wonderful. A child whose parent has died needs all the support and love he or she can get.

Foolproof Mistakes

There are no solutions that work perfectly for all the financial links remarried families have to their members and to former families. But it's simple to spot what won't work. So here's a list of foolproof mistakes that you should never, ever consider practicing.

1. Maintain two completely different standards within the same stepfamily. Especially when dealing with children, play favorites. Make no pretext about putting your kids first.

Why it doesn't work. Resident stepchildren and their parent can't help but feel offended when, after being kept on a tight financial leash throughout the year, the summertime visiting stepchildren are squired about to fancy places and treated to life's finest. The doting parent's rationale that "They're only here for such a short time" is justifiably countered by his or her spouse's reaction: "We can't be a family if everyone's entitlement is so different."

2. Skimp on the new family, spend on the old. So you're the "family destroyer," the one who initiated the divorce in your former marriage. Great. Ease the pain of your former spouse and the children by "being there" for them in dollars.

Why it doesn't work. Showering money doesn't make up for the first family's loss. And the inequality of the financial arrangement causes resentment in the remarriage.

3. Have relatives bestow lavish gifts — unequally. Encourage your children's grandparents to make a big splash of the

Honda Accord they're giving to him for his 16th birthday and tell them it's fine to send your stepdaughter a Hallmark card when she turns that "sweet" age.

Why it doesn't work. It's a resentment boiler. Of all the pressures in a remarriage, the one most difficult to control involves wealthy, generous, and loving grandparents or non-custodial parents indulging grandchildren or children with substantial gifts. When stepsiblings live together, the unequal giving is even more destructive. While it's presumptuous to tell another adult what to do with his or her money, we can encourage the generous relative to understand how their generosity breeds hostility. Perhaps they can be persuaded to make their gifts less obvious or divide the bounty more evenly.

4. Rely too heavily on a former spouse. Your entire financial well-being depends on the financial support of your former spouse.

Why it doesn't work. The ties that bind former spouses may choke the new marriage. Because money controls, the noncustodial parent who writes out hefty support checks can play all sorts of power games. He (in most cases it is he) can hold up the money because he doesn't want to send the child to private school or he can dawdle with payments just to be vindictive. If you are subject to a former spouse's whims and don't know when money will flow, then both you and your new spouse will find yourselves focusing your energies and attention on your former spouse. He's in control. You wind up taking your eyes off the main ball — forming your own financial union.

Remarried couples continuously have to rematch their funds because of the financial connections with and obligations to immediate, extended, and former family members. Fortunately, you're more knowledgeable about finances and more certain of your own financial philosophy than you were when you married for the first time. You're also less stuck in the "traditional" and more ready to search for creative solutions to the new challenges. All of that works to your advantage when you find yourself financially linked to such a wide variety of people.

Chapter 9

Remarrying after the Children Are Grown

A Healthy, Happy Prospect

DID YOU KNOW . . .

- Of those people who become widowed when they're 65 or older, fewer than 25% of the men and 1% of the women will remarry.
- Men between 45 and 64 who live alone or with someone other than a spouse are twice as likely to die within 10 years as men of the same age who live with wives. Women of this age living alone also have an increased chance of dying sooner, but not if they're in a high-income bracket.

Dr. Carl Menninger was right. Love cures people — both the ones who give it and the ones who receive it. Research confirms that remarriage among people later in life is good for the body and good for the spirit. It's true that remarriage after the death of or divorce from a long-term spouse raises new problems — many involving money. But since most money challenges have practical resolutions, it's absurd to allow money to stand in the way of less stress, greater self-esteem, and more life satisfaction — all of which widows feel when they remarry.

If, as the joke goes, life begins after the children have gone to college and the dog dies, then remarriage at this age should be extraordinary. The problem is that by the time a person is old enough to have grown children, around 55, there are 48 men to every 52 women. For women the growing imbalance is made worse because men in their age group who do remarry frequently choose women considerably younger than themselves.

Other obstacles to remarriage between older adults include society's expectations following the death of a spouse. Bereavement customarily lasts a year; widows and widowers are advised not to rush into anything; the costs — financial or emotional — of marrying another partner who may become seriously ill also weigh heavily. Moreover, public policies sometimes work to your detriment when you remarry.

Your Own Concerns

Martha, a 68-year-old wealthy widow whose deceased husband was president of a large textile company, is being told by her friends that the 58-year-old man courting her is interested only in her money.

Olga, a 59-year-old receptionist whose divorce left her with a small nest egg that she has stashed in bank CDs, fears that marrying anyone but a rich man will endanger her secure existence. So she's resisting the proposals of a 63-year-old retired teacher whom she has been seeing for three years.

Edgar, a retired 74-year-old production manager, is able to live with his woman friend comfortably on the pension and Social Security benefits he gets. He also has accumulated some savings and investments, which he has squirreled away to use only in case of health emergencies. Whatever's left he wants his son to inherit. He lives in a community property state and fears his longtime companion would get it all if they were to get married and he died first. So he's not proposing.

Vincent, a 63-year-old widower who's an executive with a major communications firm, can't seem to shake the fear that he'll be made a fool of if he marries a woman 12 years his junior. "I'm sure she'd be marrying me for my money, that she'll disappear shortly after we're married, and that the whole relationship will be a sham."

Remarriage provokes anxiety.

Both men and women question their readiness and their ability to make another commitment.

Older women, especially, worry about what they'll have to give up when they remarry. Will they sacrifice alimony (in the case of a divorce), career prospects (especially if a woman has been fending for herself successfully for quite a while and her new spouse is nearing retirement age), Social Security or pension benefits, or an adult child's emotional and financial support?

Still, many older women welcome the prospect of sharing life with a new spouse. They're eager for the companionship, sex, and financial *inter*dependence. "I've noticed that even women who have been handling their finances alone for quite a while are inclined to abdicate the responsibility when they remarry," says Chicago financial planner Susan Richards. "Many women, especially those who were married before the feminist movement, feel that making money decisions is like changing the oil in your car. You might know how to do it, but who wants to?"

There's a Lot to Talk About

The prenuptial process, that of sharing financial information, responsibilities, anxieties, goals, and dreams, is the same at 60 as it is at 30. Only the subject matter changes. Now the concentration is on what you have in the way of assets, when, if ever, you want to retire, what you'd like to retire to, and what employee and retirement benefits you can expect. You also want to know each other's financial obligations to grandchildren or adult children and your current health status and prognosis. You'll want to discuss whether you'll buy or rent a new abode, move into one of your present homes, or move in with one of the children. You'll want to know how much insurance each of you has, who the beneficiaries are, and if the insurance is appropriate in type, cost, and amount.

A Boston couple found their concerns about marriage needed to be addressed in a formal prenuptial agreement. They had known each other, off and on, for 30 years. When they lived in Boston, Mary Louise and her husband were friendly with Bob and his wife. Mary Louise and her husband moved to Virginia, and for a few years they kept in Christmas card contact with Bob's family. Then correspondence faltered. A number of years later Mary Louise divorced. Then Bob divorced. It wasn't until Mary Louise came back to Boston to go to her 35th high school reunion that she and Bob touched base again. By now Bob was confined to a wheelchair (though by no means inactive) as a result of multiple sclerosis. The genuine liking they had for one another many years ago turned into love. After a short courtship, they decided to get married. Mary Louise's adult children expressed their concern about Bob's physical condition. "I told them this is life," Mary Louise said, "and life isn't a dress rehearsal. You've got to grab on to happiness when it's presented. I know people who are handicapped in their brains, and frankly, those aren't people I want to be with. But not Bob. He's funny, kind, and exciting. I've been through too much to believe that life is an ice cream sundae that never melts. I'm going to dig in while I can."

Despite the fact that they both came into this marriage "with a commitment at least equal to that of my first marriage," says Bob, they both wanted a formal prenuptial agreement. "I was asking Mary Louise to be with me during some difficult times," Bob says. "We don't know how quickly this disease will progress. Even on days when I'm feeling well, she has to get me into my wheelchair. She's making sacrifices and I wanted her to know I appreciate them and that she'd always be taken care of. At the same time I want my pharmaceutical business to go to my children." All of that was in a prenuptial agreement.

Mary Louise had her own reasons for wanting a prenuptial. They had to do with what she was giving up when she moved to Boston — a lovely home *"that I couldn't replace here,"* a job as a well-paid dental hygienist, and income from a baby-sitting service she had started. *"It wasn't that I needed to be compensated for caring for someone I love,"* she says. *"I just needed to feel financially secure if I was going to give up working."*

Financial Obligations When There Are Health Problems

Sickness *is* always a possibility. Nobody likes to examine the prospect too closely, but the older you get, the more likely you are to have a close-up view of serious health problems. Your own and your spouse's. What, you wonder silently, will happen to your financial resources if this new love of your life needs significant and extensive long-term medical care? Nobody wants to remarry and then find himself or herself, a few years later, stripped of all but a small portion of a life savings as a result of a spouse's illness.

Obviously the chances of an extended nursing home stay are greater at 70 years of age than they are at 30. So people remarrying later in life must address the possibility — and plan for it in the hope the plans will never need to be executed.

As difficult as it is, talk about the whole health and finance issue prior to remarriage. With the help of estate planners savvy in Medicare and Medicaid eligibility and coverage, you can make provisions for yourself and your new spouse that will minimize the erosion of assets in case long-term medical care is needed.

Peter Strauss, a New York attorney who specializes in the elderly's legal concerns, outlines what people remarrying later in life might consider when they discuss finances and health.

1. Supplemental insurance planning to fill in the gaps in Medicare coverage.
2. Medicaid planning, a form of estate planning that helps an at-home spouse remain solvent if his or her spouse needs nursing home care.
3. Language in a prenuptial agreement that *might* protect you from using your money to pay for nursing home care for a spouse.

Supplemental insurance planning. While Medicare, the federal program that assists seniors and some disabled Americans with medical costs, will relieve you of some health-related expenses, there are gaps in coverage. Private insurance companies have filled in some of the cracks with supplemental coverage known as Medi-gap policies. The federal government now provides certification for all Medi-gap policies that meet certain minimum standards. Still they're confusing. Unless you're a whiz at deciphering bafflegab, seek help in choosing a Medi-gap policy. Government certification or not, all policies are not alike. Beware of waiting periods, preexisting illness exclusions, and policies that pay only a fixed amount for any treatment no matter what the actual bill.

Long-term-care insurance policies are also worth considering because home health or nursing home care is costly. A year of skilled care can cost $25,000 or more. The majority of long-term policies pay a dollar amount per day for nursing home or home health care, but that's where the similarity among policies ends. At a minimum, look for a guarantee that you can renew the policy (it would be pointless to buy a policy that won't let you renew because you're sick), coverage for all care levels (skilled care, intermediate, and home care), coverage that can't be canceled because of advancing age, a limited preexisting conditions period before coverage begins, coverage for Alzheimer's, no limitation on prior hospitalization, home health care coverage with no prior stay in a nursing home or hospital required (some illnesses are progressive, not acute).

Run from high-pressure sales tactics when buying insurance. Deal only with reputable agents and insurance companies rated A or better by Best's Reports, an independent rating firm.

Medicaid planning. This new offshoot of estate planning is even more important for people remarrying than it is for long-term marrieds (who have joint children, parallel interests and concerns, and a long history of devotion to one another). Medicaid is a joint federal/state program that provides medical assistance for people who are destitute. The goal of Medicaid planning is to keep one person solvent if the other requires expensive medical attention, such as nursing home care. It would *seem* to be a fair division in upper-middle-class homes if, in the event one spouse had to go into a nursing home, the couple were to split their assets, with half being used for the ailing person and the other half reserved for the at-home spouse who, keep in mind, may not necessarily be healthy either. (This division wouldn't be fair if the couple had very little money, however, because then the at-home spouse wouldn't have enough to live on.)

But the government has its own rules. Only a limited amount of skilled nursing care is partially paid for under Medicare. You are responsible for the rest, unless you become eligible for Medicaid. That means you must have only limited assets.

Suppose one of you has to go into a nursing home for an extended period. To understand how that affects the other's finances, you have to understand what Medicaid allows you to keep and still have your spouse qualify for Medicaid.

You can keep

- Exempt assets, which include the family home, a car, and some personal possessions such as jewelry and furs.
- A limited monthly income from pension, Social Security, or investments — and that income varies from state to state, from $815 to $1,500 (indexed for inflation).
- A portion of whatever remaining nonexempt assets the couple has (owned individually or jointly), including cash, securities, a vacation home, and other investments. The figure also varies state to state, from $12,000 to $60,000 (indexed for inflation, too).

There are a number of ways to shelter some additional assets. If the person who's sick transfers all of his or her assets to the other spouse, he or she can qualify immediately for Medicaid to pay nursing home bills. The at-home spouse can refuse to pay any of the nursing home costs, arguing that he or she needs all the money to live. Keep in mind, however, that the state has a right to seek contributions from the at-home spouse. But it has to prove the at-home spouse's statements are false.

This technique is not likely to curry favor among the ill spouse's children in a remarriage, even if it succeeds in protecting their parent's assets from the nursing home's expenses. Their inheritance now winds up in the hands of their stepparent, who may or may not distribute it to them after the death of their parent.

Another way to shelter assets is to pay off the mortgage so more of your assets are invested in the home (which is exempt from Medicaid's eligibility calculations). Medicaid laws are complex, so for a full understanding of your options, consult a planner who specializes in this type of counseling.

Prenuptial provisions. There's a trend now to insert a provision in a prenuptial agreement which says, in effect, that while you both plan to carry out the obligations to each other as spelled out in the prenuptial, you would not have married if you thought you'd have to assume the financial burden of nursing home care. The provision releases you from assuming this burden.

This provision has not been tested in the courts, and strong arguments abound that it would be in violation of public policy, which in most states says that married couples have a responsibility to one another so that they do not become welfare recipients. Attorney Peter Strauss argues that since this prenuptial agreement is signed by both parties prior to marriage, it might be upheld in court.

Move very cautiously with this one. It needs to be drafted by an elder law specialist. Even then it might not work.

A final word about the unpredictability of health. The line between good health and poor health is often fuzzy — as is the case with someone who is lucid at times and disoriented at others. You also can jump the line at a moment's notice, such as when a healthy person is brain-damaged in an auto accident. That's why it's important to have a simple legal document called a durable power of attorney. It gives another person legal authority to act for you. A durable power of attorney can be set up so that it goes into effect only if you become incapacitated. Called a "springing" durable power of attorney, it's the one many people opt for because they want control over decisions when they're healthy but need a trusted decision maker when they're incapacitated. (Make certain the definition of "incapacity" is clear and one you're comfortable with.)

It's typical for spouses to appoint one another as the attorney-in-fact or for a parent to appoint one or more trusted children. In a remarriage, the choice of attorney-in-fact may be a delicate issue because of the inherent distrust children often feel toward the new spouse. Only the person creating the durable power of attorney knows (or senses) who has the best judgment and who would act with his or her best interests at heart.

Homes

House tax rules when you're over 55. "Whose house?" is still one of the primary personal financial questions to be addressed when you remarry, whether you're in your 30s or in your 60s (see Chapter 4). But for those remarrying later, the timing of when to sell a home you've been living in for many years so that you and your new spouse can move in together packs a powerful financial wallop. The "when" determines whether you can take advantage of what may be the biggest tax break you'll ever have at your disposal. Here it is. If you're 55 or over, you may exclude up to $125,000 of gain from the sale of a principal residence, as long as you owned and lived in this home for at least three years out of the five-year period ending on the date of the sale. It wouldn't be overdoing it to hawk "This is a once in a lifetime deal," which applies even if you do not use the profits to buy a new home. You can change your mind about excluding or including the gain from profits from the sale — but at most the window of opportunity for waffling is three years.

Because profits on home sales can be rolled over — untaxed — as long as you buy a home of equal or greater value, the onetime exclusion might allow you to avoid taxes on the appreciation of all the homes you've ever owned.

The rules seem simple — until you remarry. Then they become tricky.

Suppose, for example, you sell your home in February, your fiancée sells her home in September. You marry in November and file a joint tax return for the year. If both of you met the age, ownership, and use tests at the time of your respective sales, each of you can choose to exclude $125,000 of gain ($250,000 total) if you elect to.

But here's another scenario. In February, Joe and Jill are divorced. At that time they had their jointly owned home up for sale. But real estate sales are slow and the house languishes on the market. In September Jill marries Alan. In December, Joe and Jill's home finally sells. Because they were not married to each other at the time of the sale of their home and because they meet all the tests, both Joe and Jill are eligible to take the exclusion based on the half of the home that each owned. Jill will file a return with Alan, and because he's her husband at the time, Alan must join Jill in her choice. If later, Jill dies and Alan sells their home, he cannot choose to exclude the gain again.

In another situation Arlene's husband died when she was 56 and he was 59. She stayed in their home for a couple of years, then sold it for $290,000 and rented an apartment. Since she and her deceased husband had bought the house many years ago, she had amassed quite a gain, so she opted for taking the $125,000 lifetime exclusion to reduce her taxable gain. About a year later, she met 59-year-old Charles. They fell in love. Charles owns a condo and has never taken his $125,000 lifetime exclusion. If Arlene marries Charles and moves into his condo, Charles would lose his right to his exclusion if he and Arlene decide to move later because he wouldn't be single at the time of the sale and his wife will have already taken advantage of the exclusion. But if he outlives Arlene or they divorce and *then* he sells the condo, he regains the right to the exclusion.

Instead, Arlene and Charles decide to move to another state. Charles's accountant is advising them to postpone the wedding and live together until he sells the condo, so that he can take maximum advantage of the $125,000 lifetime exclusion and save about $40,000 in taxes.

Who ever said money doesn't control mores?

The rent-versus-buy quandary. As people get older, they look to simplify their lives, not make their day-to-day existence more complicated. They contemplate selling homes and moving into condominiums or rental apartments, where maintenance is assumed by others. After you've assessed your needs and wants, remarriage at this time in your life gives you a natural opportunity to change your living arrangements. As a couple, you have to determine your overall financial position. If you have little capital or sources for future income, selling both your homes and renting an apartment and investing the accumulated equity may make sense. Too, you have to think about your life-style. If you plan to travel extensively, consider renting or buying a condo. Then mowing the lawn and cleaning the pool becomes the building management's responsibility, not yours. If, however, you're passionate about gardening and carpentry, you'll want to buy a place of your own to work on.

Protecting your spouse's right to remain in the home. A home is often the single major asset of any couple. Frequently in a remarriage a spouse wants to ensure that his or her share of this property goes, eventually, to his or her children and doesn't want the surviving spouse to be able to change that decision. But neither wants the surviving spouse squeezed out of the house when one dies simply because the heirs want or need the money and try to force a sale. One estate-planning tool frequently used to forestall that possibility is to have each spouse create a marital life estate trust that allows the surviving spouse full use of the house until his or her death. Then half the house goes to the wife's children and half to the husband's. (More about estate planning in Chapter 10.)

How Remarriage Affects Social Security and Other Benefits

The Social Security regulations are so wordy and so complex it's no wonder people are confused about what remarriage will do to their benefits.

Many a widow who has been receiving survivor's benefits from Social Security since her husband's death fears that remarriage will threaten that regular check. It won't. When you remarry you are still entitled to collect these survivor's benefits — no matter how much money your new spouse has. That's still true even if you were divorced from your now-deceased former spouse, as long as you're over age 60 and not entitled to a higher benefit based on your own earnings.

Some people are concerned that remarriage will mean that as a couple you will receive less Social Security than you would if you lived together as an unmarried couple. But that's not the case. When you're eligible for Social Security, you and your spouse will independently receive benefits based on how long each of you worked and how much you paid into the system. When you're married, you have the option of receiving benefits based on what you paid into the system, or one half of your spouse's benefits, whichever is greater.

If you remarry, don't expect to share in a *former* spouse's retirement benefits. But you can collect Social Security retirement benefits based on your *new* spouse's earnings record as long as you're over 62 or take care of your spouse's under-16-year-old (or over 16 and disabled) child. The marriage must have lasted at least one year when the wife or husband applies for benefits — or the couple must have had a child.

If your new spouse dies, you are eligible for Social Security benefits if you're over 60 (or over 50 and disabled). There are certain requirements, however. The marriage must have lasted at least nine months before your spouse died, or a shorter marriage has to have ended by accidental death, or you must have had a child together. (These requirements are designed to discourage scheming people from entering into a marriage simply to collect benefits.)

A widow who remarries but is single again due to divorce, annulment, or the death of a second husband can reapply for her first husband's veteran's benefits, assuming he was in the military.

What Will the Children Say?

Kids will be kids. Even when they're adults. The difference is that adult children's objections to the marriage will be expressed differently and will be over different issues. Rest assured, however, that there will always be one adult child who begins a conversation about your remarriage with the phrase "I know it's none of my business" and follows it with "but . . ."

Like kids, adult children resist change. It's not that their daily existence will be threatened by the introduction of a new person. It probably won't. They might be genuinely happy about the marriage. Or they simply might be relieved — relieved that they are no longer primarily responsible for the parent's emotional or financial well-being. "It has nothing to do with whether or not I like Sam," Philip says. "I like the fact that I don't have to worry about my mother daily. Sam does. I've stopped giving her the extra $300 a month that I initiated when Dad died. And quite selfishly, now my wife and I can go on vacation and not feel obligated to ask my mother to come along."

More often, however, adult children are leery or angry. Sometimes long-buried feelings of conflicting loyalties arise. In cases of divorce, it can be most evident when the adult child realizes he or she actually likes the new stepparent. When the widowed parent remarries, the child might feel guilty about treating the stepparent in the deceased parent's stead. Or incensed. "I see my father giving things to his new wife that he never gave to my mother. And she worked infinitely harder than this woman."

If all this isn't complicated enough, there are additional issues addling adult children. Some of them deal with logistics, some with behavior, most with finances.

Logistically, the new relationship throws "who's going to be where when" into chaos.

"I've always looked forward to celebrating Passover at my mother's house," Anne says. "But that's going to change as soon as she marries Murray. They're going to move to Florida [near one of his sons] and it's too expensive to fly my whole family down there each year. Besides, it wouldn't be the same."

Behaviorally, change evokes worry. Adult children don't know how they're going to establish an adult-to-adult relationship with this new person. What are they going to call him or her? They don't know what is expected from them if this person gets sick or needs their help in any way.

They don't know how this new relationship will change their parent — and in turn how it will affect their parent–adult child relationship. "My mother was always available for baby-sitting, baking, and helping me when a problem arose and I couldn't be home," Sharon, a 44-year-old divorced teacher explains. "Now she's out at the gym four mornings a week and will be taking a monthlong cruise with her new husband. It blows my mind. She's become a hip 90s woman at age 78. That's not how I envisioned these years." Sharon admits the remarriage has forced her to reflect on what she expects from her mother. "She's no longer 'on call' — which, I guess, is what I wanted from her. Too, I'm envious. She has renewed vitality and the time, money, and mate to do pretty much what she wants."

Change also can push an adult child to reassess his or her own marriage. "I know it sounds crazy," Bea says, "but I was so frightened of change that I figured I'd just have to live with my husband until he died, just as my mother had with my father. My mother's choice to marry again gave me the courage I needed to make a change. Instead of sitting at home waiting for my former husband to be killed in an accident, and feeling guilty about having those thoughts, I decided to take matters into my own hands. I divorced him. Although I haven't remarried yet, I now believe I have a chance to meet someone who is kind and caring — just like Mom did."

Adult children often like their parent's intended. Sometimes they know the person well because he or she is a longtime family friend or because the person is kind to the parent. However, they become suspicious when they think this new person will take advantage of their parent.

All eyes rivet on the woman who marries a younger man or a man who marries a younger woman, for example. "Adult children may see this as exploitive — whether or not it is," says Dr. Florence Kaslow, director of the Florida Couples and Family Institute in West Palm Beach. "In the case of the older woman, people ask 'Why would he want to marry someone older unless it's for her money?' and in the case of the older man, it's 'She's only after him for his money or his status.' When a person marries someone closer in age and in net worth, there's not as much distrust."

A New York City attorney tells of a visit from a 45-year-old son of a 78-year-old widower who was planning to marry a woman 18 years his junior. "This woman is coarse and crude — a real sharpie," the son confided to the attorney. "A gold digger who only wants my father's money. I've asked him to call you to discuss a prenuptial."

The 78-year-old came in to talk about a prenuptial agreement. He wanted to put about a third of his estate into a trust that his new wife could draw on for as long as she lived. The rest of his estate would go to his son.

When the attorney mentioned the son's objections to the

marriage, the father replied, "I never had it so good. She's fun, exciting, and makes me feel 20 years younger. I know it will cost me, but what better way to spend my money. Far better than on medicine and a nursing home."

Issues of finance and inheritance seem to stir up the most concern. How will the marriage affect the support an adult child is getting? (One in three adults in their 20s receives some financial help from parents.) What will the remarriage mean to inheritance? What will become of family heirlooms or even ordinary objects with sentimental value? Will the adult child continue to provide some financial support to a parent who's remarrying?

"It's a complicated question of accountability when you're contemplating a remarriage and have adult children," says Boston attorney Mark Levinson. "It's as if you had these children looking over your shoulder and you had to seek their permission to marry — obliquely or directly." Certainly in the case of a remarriage more parents will solicit the opinions of their adult children than they would of young children. And they listen more carefully to any objections raised, even when the children are infinitely more conservative with their parents than they would be for themselves.

What Do You Owe Children?

People in their 50s, 60s, and 70s often consider financial information private and balk at the thought of sharing inheritance matters with their children. In a simple family situation where two parents split their estate between two children who feel equally loved and are in the same socio-economic bracket, perhaps nothing need be said. The will would speak for itself. But we're talking about remarriage. Remarriage means you're bringing another person, often a complete stranger, into the family picture. Understand that whatever you think of this new union, the children don't see it as important as the one in which they were conceived.

And in the case of inheritance, adult children expect money or property to follow a bloodline, not a wedding band. They will probably refer to you as "my mother's husband" or "my father's wife" rather than "my stepfather" or "my stepmother" — further drawing the psychological distinction between blood and marriage. Whether it's conscious or not, everyone realizes that the relationship between the "steps" will take longer to develop than when children are younger, mainly because there's less time together.

Assuming you have a good relationship with your adult children, you owe them time to talk over their concerns and expectations — and yours.

You're not alone if you have to clear your throat and take a deep breath before you discuss the dollars and cents of inheritance. It's a subject that evokes powerful emotions — even in first marriages. It raises several uncomfortable issues that are difficult to maneuver around: death, money, and how children are perceived by their parents. Throw a new spouse into the mix and a province already rife with symbolism and ambiguity becomes more so.

Yet the goal is to avoid the mistrust that comes with not knowing.

For anyone to urge universal disclosure of estate plans or inheritance to children would be imprudent. We have different relationships with each child. They, too, are different from one another. We have to know our own children. They are, after all, still people, people who fall all over the spectrum between caring and crass, selfless and selfish, generous and greedy. A grasping daughter will probably become more grasping when she hears about the remarriage. An adaptable son will be more amenable to the idea. "Jonathan and Abbey are terrific people and I'd tell them everything about my finances," Rochelle says. "But Lila, she's different. I haven't spoken to her for five years. I owe her nothing, not even talk."

Children with whom you have a good relationship deserve to know where they stand, emotionally and financially, as a result of this marriage. If the family relationship has been a fairly harmonious one, you'll be surprised how effective the trust you've built up will be in relieving the anxiety surrounding the topic.

Acknowledging your children's involvement by soliciting their opinions does not mean you give them decision-making authority over your life — no matter how much respect you have for them. And it's inappropriate for them to demand it. "Sometimes I'm appalled by adults who treat their parents as children, threatening not to have anything to do with the parent if he or she remarries," says one Atlanta attorney. "These kids never treated their parents well to begin with and are only concerned they'll be nosed out of an inheritance. I want to jump across the table and scream to these parents that they don't have to listen to their kids or allow themselves to be bullied."

After they're widowed, it is natural for people to be concerned about protecting their assets for the children. But that's *their* choice. Not the kids'. There's nothing written anywhere that says you have to leave your children a hefty inheritance.

"I've always told my children 'I've given you a college education and whatever money I can afford for a down payment on your houses,' " says Larsen, a real estate broker in Minneapolis. "That's what I felt I owed them. Nothing more. Yet," he continues, "that doesn't mean I don't want them to inherit anything. When I married for the third time I told them we had worked out an agreement which says anything I earned before our marriage goes to them, anything Gretchen earned [as a doctor] before our marriage goes to her children. Anything we earn from now on goes to each other — to do with what we want."

Most people do feel an emotional bonding with their

children — strong enough that they'd like to leave them some inheritance and no financial indebtedness.

Allaying Children's Inheritance Jitters

Naturally, even before you discuss the subject of inheritance with your children, you should discuss it with your intended or new spouse, who should be aware of your financial loyalties, concerns, and obligations. You may have told your daughter she'll be inheriting your art collection. You may have promised your granddaughter you'll give her the money she'll need to buy into a dental practice. You and your siblings may send your elderly mother additional support payments each month. Or as part of a separation agreement, you may have an insurance policy naming your former spouse as beneficiary. Make it clear to your fiancé that you have an ethical commitment to uphold these financial promises, that the commitment is not in conflict with the love you have for him or her.

Prenuptial agreements are recommended for remarrieds with substantial assets simply because you've spent a great deal of time building them (usually with a former spouse), and should they evaporate, there is less time to rebuild them.

Once the two of you have a fair understanding of how you plan to allocate assets now *and* after you die, you might want to call a family gathering (one family at a time, please).

If you have drawn up a prenuptial, paint a broad picture of what's in it to your adult children.

If you haven't, but are in the process of drawing up a will (universally recommended when you remarry), tell them what you hope to accomplish. Adult children should know the rationale behind your decisions, especially if they are not the immediate beneficiaries of your estate or you have done something unusual with your property or the estate is not divided equally among the children.

If, for example, you have created a marital life estate trust, which ensures that your property will eventually go to the children, tell them why you've done this. ''While we have bought our house as tenants in common, which means my share can be left to you immediately, I want to make certain that Millie is able to live in our home for the remainder of her life. She wants the same thing for me. What we've done is set up a trust that allows that. When we both are gone, my half will go to my children, her half to hers.'' (Many different types of control can be imposed on these trusts. The trustee can be someone other than the surviving spouse. The trustee might be required to make periodic reports to the final beneficiaries, the adult children. The spouse can be prohibited from selling any property in the marital life estate trust.)

Or suppose you've lent your stepdaughter $15,000 for a down payment on a home, but you intend to forgive the loan if it's not repaid at the time of your death. You might tell your children, so they understand your motives. ''If Nicole can't repay the $15,000, my will is going to forgive her. I wanted her to have the house and she has not been able to build up the financial reservoir that you have. I know you'll understand that this gift doesn't affect my deep love for you.''

You might consider naming one of your adult children a coexecutor or a cotrustee. It can be with your spouse (if the relationship is fairly stable) or someone else. By giving a child this responsibility, you're sending the message that you respect this person and have confidence in him or her.

Gifts: Now May Be a Better Time Than Later

Talking about inheritance presents a wonderful opportunity for adult children to be asked what objects have symbolic value to them, what objects they would like to have — either now or later when the parent dies. Such a meeting among one family resulted in one of the sons hauling away to his own home his mother's armoire and a daughter leaving with the portrait of her parents that she had always loved. The new wife was secretly delighted. "We had no room for the armoire in our new co-op and I really didn't care to have the painting around," she confides.

Gift giving (while we're well and able to experience the joy of the recipient) can be great fun. It can also be very reassuring to adult children whose parents are remarrying. If they were conditioned to equate money and love, they feel bolstered by the gift. If they are in need of it, they don't feel that the new relationship will mean financial abandonment.

People who can afford it can give up to $10,000 annually to as many people as they want without having to pay a gift tax. (As a couple you can give $20,000.) If gifts are made each year, this $10,000/$20,000 annual exclusion can achieve substantial estate-tax savings for heirs later on.

If you don't want to or can't give money, making a gift of life insurance to a child can substantially reduce or eliminate federal estate taxes. The life insurance given is a policy you own on your own life. To keep it out of your estate, the policy must be given at least three years before your death. The value of the insurance policy at the time of the gift is subject to gift tax, but that's far less than the amount the policy will pay at your death. If you own the policy, the proceeds are included in your taxable estate. If your child owns it (which means he or she has to pay premiums), they are not.

Aside from the $10,000/$20,000 annual exemption, there are other transfers of money or property that are exempt from gift tax. Of special interest to remarrieds are gifts between spouses, and payment of medical bills (to relatives or friends) or of school tuition (to assist grandchildren).

At Last, Another Choice

"Here's a dilemma we never thought about when we were first married," Herman said. "Where are we going to be buried?"

Herman and Flo, both 71, are not alone. Though they laugh about this new wrinkle in their six-year-old remarriage, theirs is a frequent predicament among those who remarry later in life.

Most remarriages after 60 involve at least one widow or widower. Their first marriages might have been very happy. At the time of the first spouse's death, the surviving spouse probably had every intention of being buried near or next to his or her spouse someday.

When the widow remarries and spends many happy years with a new spouse, the "plot plot" thickens.

Children of the first marriage might express strong feelings about wanting their parents to be buried together. "And that's understandable," says Flo (who is more concerned about the dilemma than Herman). "I feel it's important to consider their wishes."

The couple also feels pulled in two directions. Herman, who was a bachelor before marrying Flo, could be buried in a family plot but would prefer to buy a plot for Flo and himself. She's not sure she wants that; she's vacillating between being buried near her first husband and being buried near Herman. They have not yet come to any decisions. "Believe it or not, I'm thinking of cremation," says Flo. "I may have half my ashes buried with my first husband and half buried with Herman."

Up to the very end, remarrieds must come up with creative solutions to peculiar problems.

Chapter 10

Estate Planning
Assets, Heirlooms — and What About the Kids?

✧ ✧ ✧

DID YOU KNOW . . .
- A husband and wife cannot disinherit each other — except if they both agree to it in writing.
- Between 80 and 90% of parents with young children have no formal instructions specifying who will care for the children in the event of the parents' death.

By the time people reach remarrying age, they usually don't ask THE question: "Why worry about estate planning if I don't have an 'estate'?" They know the answer.

"I'm not sure if we have 'assets,' or 'stuff,' but we do have kids and we have to make certain that everyone and everything is accounted for — eventually," says Kathie, a Miami physician remarried for eight years.

Nor by this time are people any longer likely to be comforted by the notion that they're too young to die. They usually know of at least one contemporary who has died — either in an accident or from an untimely illness.

Yet they stall when it comes to estate planning.

Merely owning up to a need for estate planning doesn't propel a couple into action. In a candid admission to a group of remarried couples some years ago, Fern Topas Salka, a Los

Angeles matrimonial lawyer whose specialty is counseling stepfamilies, said, "I counsel clients on the need for an estate plan. I lecture on its importance. Yet I, myself, have not adequately redesigned my estate plan to take into account my present stepfamily arrangement. I can't face up to it, even though my husband urges me to. As soon as I think about redrafting my will, I come face to face with many difficult loyalty issues which exist in our family. Who will take care of my children? Who will get my money? Who will live in my house?"

Even if you haven't met with an estate planner (who can be a lawyer, a trained financial planner, a Certified Life Underwriter [CLU], or an accountant specially trained in this field), you probably have done some estate planning. You have a named beneficiary on your insurance policy. The house deed lists you as owner. The safe-deposit box at the bank is in joint name. You own the car you drive; your spouse owns the other. Perhaps a separation agreement you signed requires you to leave some portion of your estate to your children from a prior marriage. Perhaps your spouse has a bank account in trust for a child.

Whether planned or patched together, you have an estate plan.

For remarrieds, reconstruction isn't easy. Splintered loyalties, new responsibilities, and changed needs force remarried couples to create estate plans that are the paper equivalents of Rube Goldberg's mechanical contrivances. Plans must take into consideration the makeup of this new, complicated family, the assets of the spouses, their goals, and the best way to put the pieces together so that the aims are accomplished. And they must ensure that each spouse has complete control over how his or her property is distributed after death — as complete as the law and prior agreements allow.

Who's Kin?

Before planning a meeting with an estate planner, draw up a list of family members for whom you have financial responsibility, both legally and morally. It gives you a visual idea of the scope of the family. It also provides the estate planner with a scorecard of who's who in your family.

"ABOUT THE FAMILY" Worksheet

For your convenience, prepare a separate chart for each of you.

Your Personal Information

1. Name _____
   Address _____
   Phone number _____
   Any other names you've had _____
2. Occupation _____
   Business address _____
   Phone number _____
3. Social Security number _____
4. Date and place of birth _____
5. This marriage: date and place _____
6. Prior marriages:
   name and address of former spouse _____
   date and place of marriage _____
   date and reason for its ending (death or divorce)
   _____

Your Children from Prior Marriages

	First	Second	Third
1. Name	_____	_____	_____
Date of birth	_____	_____	_____
Place of birth	_____	_____	_____

2. Address　　　　　_____　_____　_____
3. Social Security
   number　　　　　_____　_____　_____
4. Explanation of
   present support
   arrangements
   (if child is still
   dependent)　　　_____　_____　_____
5. If independent
   and applicable
   Occupation　　　_____　_____　_____
   Name of his or
   her spouse　　　　_____　_____　_____
   Name of children　_____　_____　_____

Your Children from This Marriage

	First	Second	Third
1. Name	_____	_____	_____
Date of birth	_____	_____	_____
Place of birth	_____	_____	_____
2. Social Security number	_____	_____	_____

Other Dependents

1. Name	_____	_____
Address	_____	_____
2. Relationship	_____	_____
3. Age	_____	_____
4. Present support arrangements	_____	_____

The Visual Picture of Your Family

A remarried family can get complicated. There are relatives, step-relatives, and quasi-kin (a former spouse's new husband or wife and his or her blood kin). There is often a confusion as to the family's boundaries. For example, are children who "visit" considered part of the new family and are they to be treated as custodial children? Who has more influence on a child's life — a noncustodial father or a custodial stepfather?

Save some legal fees by providing your estate planner with a geneogram (like an extended family tree) that distinguishes the most immediate members of this new family and shows their relationship to each other and to you. It goes beyond stating the legal obligations; it visualizes the emotional and physical ties.

Start by placing yourself and your spouse in the center — boldly — since you are the linchpins for this family. (Males are represented by squares; females by circles.)

From there, branch up for your parents. Dip down for your children. If there are grandchildren, drop them below children. Sisters and brothers (and their children) spin off above and to the side of you. Place ages within the boxes. (An x through a circle or square indicates the person has died.)

Marriages are represented by a solid line (———); divorces by a solid line slashed by two diagonal lines (—//—); separations with a solid line slashed by a single diagonal line (—/—); and living together but not married with a broken line (- - - -).

In the accompanying geneogram, both Gerald and Heidi have been married once before and each has one sibling. She has three children from a prior marriage; he, two. Both of their former spouses have remarried, though Gerald's former wife, Ellen, is divorced again.

The large, dotted, bootlike shape indicates those who are living in Gerald and Heidi's household.

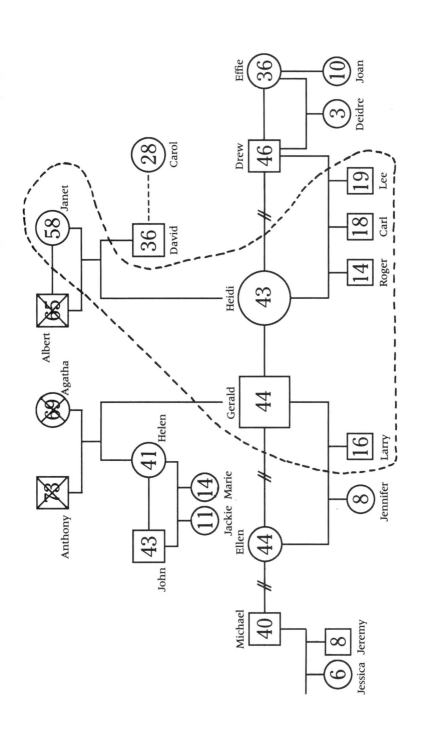

Who Owns What

You can't give away what you don't own. So before making estate plans, inventory your major possessions. Key in this exercise is knowing what the different forms of ownership mean. (Many states have slight variations of wording, so check with your attorney if you have a question.) A brief review:

Joint tenancy. Each joint tenant owns an equal share of the property with all other joint tenants. The share of the first tenant to die *must* go to the remaining joint tenants, even if there's a will to the contrary.

Community property. In the eight community property states (Arizona, California, Idaho, Nevada, New Mexico, Texas, Washington, and Wisconsin), any property a spouse earns or acquires during a marriage becomes the property of the marriage (with a few exceptions), which means each of you owns half the property. Each of you can leave your one-half share of community property to whoever you want. The other half belongs to your spouse. You have no right to give that away.

Separate property. This is defined differently depending on whether you live in a community property state or in a common law property state. In community property states, all property that isn't community property is held separately. In common law property states, separate property means all property each spouse owns individually — unless there is a written contract to the contrary.

Tenancy in common. In this shared ownership, you can leave your portion of the property held as tenants in common to whoever you choose, unless restricted by a contract. Unlike in joint tenancy, with tenancy in common the owners' shares do not have to be equal.

Partnership. Property that is owned by business partners. Most partnerships have an agreement stating how a partner's financial interests will be handled in event of death.

Corporate shares. The bylaws of a corporation or a shareholders' agreement generally dictate how the shares in a closely held or small corporation are handled in case of a shareholder's death.

With this information in hand, you're ready to tackle the "What We Own" worksheet. Don't get stalled with insignificant details. An estimate, not an assessment, is all you need for the Net Value (the estimated worth minus any debt on the property) column.

"WHAT WE OWN" Worksheet

END:
Joint tenancy   TC = Tenants in common
= Community property   P = Partnership
W = Husband's property or wife's property   CS = Corporate shares

Description of Property	Type of Ownership	Percentage You Own	NET VALUE		
			Husband	Wife	Joint
ETS					
king accounts					
1gs accounts					
ey market funds or :counts					
1al funds					
ficates of deposit (CDs)					
rnment bonds					
<s					
1s					
ous metals					

Description of Property	Type of Ownership	Percentage You Own	NET VALUE		
			Husband	Wife	Joint
Automobiles (and any other vehicles, such as boats, planes)					
Art, antiques, or valuable furniture					
Jewelry, furs					
Money owed to you					
Shares of limited partnerships; vested interests in profit-sharing plans and stock options; vested interests in retirement plans such as IRAs, Keoghs, annuities					
Cash value in life insurance policies					
Other personal property of value					
REAL ESTATE					
(Fill in addresses; subtract the amount you owe on your mortgage from the projected selling price of the property to get the net value)					
Home					
Second home					
Investment property					
BUSINESS PROPERTY					
Business ownership(in sole proprietorship, partnership, corporation)					

"WHAT MY ESTATE GOALS ARE"
Worksheet

Name_____

I want to . . .

____ provide security for my surviving spouse.

____ be certain my children have a guardian of my choosing.

____ provide money to be used for children's education.

____ keep the business in the family.

____ assure the continuity of the business.

____ make certain my money and assets eventually wind up with my children from a former marriage.

____ provide our child with the same (or similar) financial benefits that my older children had.

____ treat heirs equitably (not necessarily equally).

____ provide for the special needs of a particular heir.

____ provide support for my elderly parent(s).

____ designate certain items (from heirlooms to "stuff") for certain heirs.

____ eliminate certain potential heirs from receiving any property from me.

____ protect my property from medical/nursing home costs.

____ leave a certain amount or a portion of my estate to a charity or organization.

____ (my particular goals)

____

____

Yet Wills Are Important

So why all the pressure to draw up a will? Why do lawyers look askance at people who don't have them? Why does Dick Dunn, who heads the stepfamily ministry at the Roswell Methodist Church in Roswell, Georgia, insist that before he counsels people considering a remarriage they begin drawing up a will?

"The complications of one or both of the spouses in a subsequent marriage dying without a will are too great," says Reverend Dunn. What can cause the complications?

Children. Dependent children are the primary reason to have a will. As a parent, you want to have a say about who's going to rear them and look after the property you're leaving to them. You're dealing with your most valuable asset. Decisions of such major importance shouldn't be made by an arbitrary state law.

Everything you haven't accounted for elsewhere. Suppose you have things of value — sentimental or real — that you want to give to certain people or organizations. Or you won the lottery or came into an unexpected inheritance and you died before you had time to give it away or put it in a trust? Again, without a will, state law dictates how that property would be distributed.

State laws differ. If you die without a will, your spouse and your children usually are the beneficiaries — though the percentages of what each gets varies state by state. And children are all treated equally — whether they are children of a first marriage or children of a remarriage. That makes it especially difficult on young, dependent children who need greater financial support than adult children. If you have no children, some of your property might go to your parents. If you want to know exactly how your state handles intestacy (dying without a will), leaf through your state's legal code, which is available at a public or law library. Or speak to an attorney.

For remarrieds, things can get messy if an old will is in effect when you die. While states wouldn't allow your present spouse to be disinherited (in effect, revoking the claims of a former spouse), any specific gifts made to your former spouse might still go to him or her. If, for example, you specifically named your former wife in a will you made many years ago as the beneficiary of farmland that has been in your family for centuries, and you never destroyed or revoked the old will, she might become "mistress of the meadows" — even if that's the last thing you'd want.

Even when you've carefully plotted out who gets what, time has a way of altering those Solomon-like judgments. "I inherited a whole slew of antiques," Jack explains. "I wanted them to stay in the family, so in my will I left them to my children — since Cassy and I have no children together. We've been married about 14 years now and my kids have told me they hate the antiques. So I'm changing my will again. Cassy gets all of them. She can do with the pieces whatever she wants. If she remarries and her new husband winds up with them, it's fine with me."

Who's going to take care of the custodial children? This is often the toughest question you'll face when preparing a will.

Under normal circumstances when one parent dies the other biological parent assumes custody of the children. Even after a divorce. But remarriage often challenges this assumption. In all probability, for instance, a 10-year-old child who has been living with her mother, stepfather, and half sister for six years will be shipped off to live with her biological father after her mother's death. That's assuming he wants her and is capable of caring for her. Capable means competent; it doesn't mean that parent is the better of the two men (father and stepfather) to do the job of child rearing. And it doesn't take into consideration the needs of the child who might be much better off in the bosom of a caring and familiar stepfather and half sister during this traumatic time.

"I cringe to think that Eliot might someday have custody of the children," says Madeline of her former husband. "To me he's a religious lunatic, cheap beyond belief, mean, dishonest, and unstable. It's especially repugnant because the children really love Glen and feel as if *he's* their real dad. But my separation agreement has me locked into naming Eliot as guardian. If nothing else, that's reason enough to keep me alive and healthy until the children are adults," Madeline jokes, halfheartedly.

Wills generally should not violate anything you've already agreed to in a separation or prenuptial agreement. In Madeline's case, however, she might try naming Glen as the children's guardian in her will and hope Eliot won't contest the custody choice in court if she dies while the children are still minors. If he does, her case for violating the separation agreement would be strengthened if in the will or in an attached note to the will she explains her reasons. They would have to be more than a personal vendetta if she wanted the court to overturn the separation agreement. Powerful arguments would be that the absent parent hadn't provided support, hadn't seen the child for years, had a history of alcohol or drug abuse, was mentally unstable or physically abusive. Even if a father were any of those things, however, there is no guarantee the court would decide against his guardianship in a contested battle. A stepparent still has no legal standing with regard to stepchildren. But in current custody decisions, more and more judges consider the length of the remarriage, how involved the biological father has remained in the children's lives, what the children want, and what is perceived to be the best interests of the children.

The process of naming guardians for custodial children in a remarriage is similar to the way it's done in a first marriage.

- You name someone you trust to rear your children in a manner you'd approve.
- You make certain you choose someone who is willing, ready, and able to do the job. And discuss it with him or her first.
- You name an alternate guardian, in case at the time of your death the primary guardian can't assume the responsibility or in the event you and the primary guardian die at the same time.

Who's going to manage the property (money and investments) you leave to a minor child?

In most cases, the person to whom you have entrusted the child's physical and emotional care is the person you'd want to control the child's money — even if that person is a former spouse. That's because you assume the property would be used honestly to provide for the child's normal living expenses and health and education needs.

But — and this is a big "but" — what if one of the reasons you and your former spouse divorced was because you couldn't tolerate each other's handling of or attitudes about money? In that case, you'd probably want to name another person to act as your child's property manager. That person may or may not be your present spouse, depending on whether the web of emotions surrounding the remarriage is entangled with bitterness and revenge. It would also depend on whether your present spouse could or would want to have a continuing relationship — albeit a financial one — with your former spouse.

Prior orders. Sometimes there is something in a will that contradicts an earlier agreement.

Often the agreement was signed so long ago, people forget about it or don't think it's still in force.

Sometimes people deliberately try to slip something into a will that counters an agreement because the agreement is onerous to them.

Unless the prior agreement is deemed illegal or no longer valid, it prevails and takes precedent over the will.

What to take to the lawyer's office. You can draw up your own will. Yet even in the simplest "no children — no assets" remarriage, it's safest to seek the counsel of an estate attorney.

Choose an attorney you feel comfortable with, because as Atlanta estate attorney Ann Salo says, "Though I deal in a very narrow band of a person's life, I share intimate details about family and finances. The shingle I really need is the one that says 'estate therapist.' "

Stuff the following into your briefcase after you've chosen your estate therapist and are ready to draw up a will:

- the "What We Own" worksheet
- the "About the Family" worksheet and, if you drew one, your geneogram
- the "What My Estate Goals Are" worksheet
- copies of previous wills, if any
- insurance policies
- divorce or separation decrees, if any
- any prenuptial agreement
- tax returns for the past three years (one of the best methods of determining all your assets)
- deferred compensation contracts, pension, or profit-sharing agreements

Before signing a will, reexamine your estate goals worksheet to be certain that your primary goals are reflected in the entire estate plan, including your will.

The Probate Panic

Why do people shudder when probate is mentioned? Though it sounds like an ominous procedure, it's simply a legal process by which a court approves your will and formally appoints the executor you've named, who then oversees the distribution of your property. The proceedings are generally mere formalities unless the will is contested or it's hard to locate the people who might have an interest in the estate if you had died intestate (without a will).

What causes the initial shudder is that most people have heard horror stories about how long the process takes. It needn't take more than a few months, but it can take years if there are snags. Also, people are concerned about the cost of probate. The larger the estate the executor has to administer, the larger the commission he or she receives from that estate (although if the executor is also a beneficiary, that can be a plus — tax-wise). Lawyers generally charge on an hourly rate, rather than as a percentage of the estate.

There are a number of estate planning vehicles that move assets out of the probate loop — life insurance, gifts, trusts, joint ownership, bank accounts — all of which will be discussed shortly. One thing you must keep in mind: avoiding probate doesn't mean your estate avoids estate tax. If tax is applicable, it has to be paid, whether your assets are probated or not.

Talk About Trusts

"It's curious that the word trust when it's used in connection with estate planning connotes a lack of trust," writes John Levy, executive director of the Jung Institute in San Francisco and an expert in the psychology of inheritance. But it shouldn't. Certainly not among husbands and wives in remarriages. Trusts can be helpful in managing and protecting property for the person you want to benefit. Some trusts can be set up within the framework of your will; others operate outside of it. And some sidestep probate.

Let's look at some trusts that can solve problems for remarrieds.

The living trust. To those of us who think of a trust as an instrument that springs to life after death, this oxymoron is as appealing as a ghoul. So I prefer to speak of a living trust by its more palatable name, a revocable trust. While you live, you still effectively own all the property you transfer to your revocable trust and do with it what you want — keep it, sell it, spend it, or give it away. When you die, the trust becomes operational and all the property passes to the people or organizations named in the trust.

For some, living trusts are unnecessary. A young couple with relatively few assets probably just needs life insurance and a will, which is less costly to draft than a trust.

But other people should consider living trusts: those with estates exceeding $600,000 who want to avoid probate, those who want their assets distributed promptly when they die, or those who want to make the distribution of their assets more difficult to contest.

The Q-Tip trust. This formidable estate planning tool, the qualified terminable interest property trust, can be used only by spouses and is especially useful for remarried couples. Its main purpose is to postpone payment of estate taxes that would otherwise be due when one spouse dies. But it has an added advantage. It allows you to make certain your spouse has the full or partial use of your property for as long as he or she lives, but permits you to name the ultimate beneficiaries when your spouse dies.

The discretionary trust. When there is a disabled child in the family, planners often suggest a trust that gives the trustee (the person or people who manage the trust) discretion to use the principal and income as is seen fit to meet the beneficiary's needs. The trustee is not required, however, to expend income or principal for the care, health, and education of the disabled child — which means the child doesn't lose government benefits.

Bank Accounts Can Be Made into Informal Trusts

It's refreshing to be able to report on a little-known estate planning device within banks that's simple and cost free to establish. Known by a variety of names ("informal trusts," "pay-on-death accounts," "bank trust accounts," and "Totten trusts," to name a few), these accounts allow you complete control over the funds in them for as long as you live. You can establish a new account with this trust designation or you can convert an existing account. All you do is set up an account, in your name, as depositor and as "trustee for the benefit of (your beneficiary)." After you die, all the beneficiary needs to do to get the money is present the bank with proof of his or her identity and a certified copy of your death certificate.

Keep in mind that while this trust avoids probate it is still part of the taxable estate and will not save on federal or state death taxes, assuming your estate is large enough to have to pay them.

Joint Tenancy Avoids Probate, But . . .

We talked about joint tenancy with the right of survivorship in Chapter 4, "Your Home," because homes bought by married couples are frequently owned in this form. But bank accounts, even businesses, can be owned as joint tenants. And that means when one joint tenant dies, his or her ownership share is automatically transferred to the surviving joint tenant, without having to go through the probate process.

Owning property as a joint tenant doesn't eliminate the property from your taxable estate for federal estate-tax purposes. However, if husband and wife are joint tenants, only one half of the value of the joint tenancy property is included in the taxable estate of the first spouse to die.

There are other tax concerns, though, the most important being the federal income tax basis rules. The concepts are complex and differ depending on whether or not you live in a community property state. They need to be worked through with an accountant or an estate planner. The general rule of thumb is that it doesn't pay, tax-wise, to transfer substantially appreciated property (or property that may substantially appreciate) into joint tenancy with your spouse if you are likely to die first.

Life Insurance Is a Boon

Life insurance is a wonderful estate planning tool. It is a simple and inexpensive way to protect all the dependents of young stepfamilies (assuming you're in good health and do not have to pay an inflated premium). As I mentioned before, it is also a way of avoiding probate — because the proceeds of the policy go directly to the beneficiary named in the policy. That's important because after your death there will be debts to pay and lost income. Your beneficiary probably will need the ready cash.

Since the proceeds are not subject to probate, only the executor of your estate needs to know about the money so he or she can file the federal estate-tax return. Sometimes the less known the better, especially, for example, in remarriages when there may be resentment among children about what their biological parent is leaving his or her spouse. The law considers husbands and wives one financial entity and says you can move property — in life as in death — to each other free of estate or gift tax. That includes life insurance proceeds.

Proceeds from life insurance are generally income tax free — no matter if you or someone else owns the policy on your life. If you, the insured, own the policy, the proceeds are considered part of your estate and may mean, depending on the size of the estate, that estate taxes might have to be paid if the beneficiary or beneficiaries are anyone but your spouse. If you don't own the policy (say, your children own a policy on your life), the proceeds from the policy are still not subject to income taxes, and may escape estate taxes.

Insurance solves problems. Suppose, for example, an older man marries a younger woman, about the age of his children. He and she have children together. The husband wants his wife and second family to inherit most of his estate. The problem is that the estate consists primarily of his family business and the wife doesn't want to be involved in the business.

While alive the husband transfers some equity to his older children, who are working in the business. This can be done without losing control. Insurance fills in the rest of the puzzle. The husband buys a large insurance policy on his life naming his wife as beneficiary. He leaves his share of the business to his adult children. There might be a large estate tax on the value of the business, since property left to children (or anyone other than a spouse) is heavily taxed after a $600,000 exemption. Therefore, the children should own a life insurance policy on the father — enough to cover the tax due.

Or perhaps a stepfather wants to leave money to his stepchildren without his children finding out. If the stepchildren are the owners of the life insurance policy (the stepfather can always give them money to cover the cost of the premiums), proceeds from the policy are kept out of his taxable estate. Insurance is a quiet way of leaving money to heirs.

There's little doubt about the value of insurance in estate

planning. The dilemma usually spins around what to buy. Consider this valuable rule of thumb: If a person expects to hold the insurance for less than 10 years, he or she should buy term. Longer than that, consider permanent insurance.

Term insurance. Term, the cheapest form of coverage, provides a preset amount of cash if the insured dies while the policy is in force. If you live beyond the term of the policy (and don't renew it), you get no money. It doesn't build up a recoverable cash value. Term is excellent for people with young families because the younger the insured the more reasonable the premiums. As you get older there is a steep increase in rates because you have a greater chance of dying. Choose a policy that will be renewable at the end of its term, in case you want to keep it in force. If you think you'd want to convert a term policy into a whole life or universal policy one day, look for that feature.

Whole life. This type of insurance, which goes by a slew of other names, most frequently "straight life," supplies a set amount of coverage for fixed, uniform premiums — but also has a savings feature, called a cash reserve, which earns interest. While you're living, you can cash in the reserve or borrow against it.

Compared to term insurance, whole life requires a much greater outlay when you're in your 20s, 30s, or 40s. There comes a point, though (and it differs company by company) when whole life's flat rate is less than term's increasing premiums. That's why it doesn't pay to buy whole life for just a few years when you're under 40.

Universal life. A hybrid of term and whole life, universal life, like whole life, builds up a cash reserve at competitive interest rates. But it's flexible. You can vary premium payments or the amount of coverage, or both, from year to year, which is a boon to most remarrieds because each year's financial picture is so different.

Gifts to Minor Children

If you're one of those fortunate people who is financially secure and generous, you can reduce your estate by distributing part of it to your own minor children or stepchildren. Except for a small amount (between $2,500 and $5,000 depending on the state) any property given to a minor must be supervised by an adult. If the gift is for your own child who is living with your former spouse with whom you have a good relationship, the simplest way to make the gift is to give it to the custodial parent outright. Says one Philadelphia nurse remarried for the third time, "Just because I found my first husband frightfully boring doesn't mean he isn't a good father. Nobody cares more about my kids than he does."

Or you could establish a simple trust, say, a bank account, under the terms of the Uniform Transfers to Minors Act in your state. As soon as you transfer funds to this account, the money is locked in. The account belongs to and is taxed to the child. You can't withdraw money if you need it and the funds can only be used for the child's welfare while he or she is still a minor. After that, the money is the child's — to do with as he or she chooses. You can make gifts to stepchildren and biological children this way. And you can choose anyone to be trustee — your former spouse, your present spouse, or even a grandparent.

There are also some investments for children that make tax sense: zero-coupon bonds, tax-exempt municipal bonds, or bond funds; Series EE U.S. Savings bonds. The savings bonds have become a real lifesaver in the saving-for-college struggle. If that's the motive behind the gift, buy them for yourself (if you're the parent) or your spouse (if you're the stepparent) or your children (if you're the grandparent). If the bonds are cashed in during the year that college tuition is being paid, the parent won't have to pay tax on the accumulated interest (assuming the parent's adjusted gross income is not too high).

Keep in mind that you can give annual gifts of up to $10,000 per person to as many people as you'd want without having to pay any gift tax. More on gifts in Chapter 9, "Remarrying after the Children Are Grown."

What to Tell the Kids?

Death may be a difficult subject for adults; but it's the stuff of nightmares for children. While most experts suggest talking to school-age children about the aspects of your death that concern them the most — such as responding to the question, "Who's going to take care of me, Mommy or Sheila?" — the details of a will or estate plan are too complicated and would only raise their anxieties. When children are old enough, they might be asked to share their thoughts, say on whom they'd rather live with, their stepfather or Aunt Alexandra. Involving the children doesn't mean you're going to abide by their wishes. It means you respect their opinions and will consider them when making your decisions.

Fitting the Pieces Together

One family's his-and-their children. "It took us about a year to smooth out the rough edges in our individual plans," says Samantha, a 38-year-old Illinois mother of a toddler who had been married to Dick for seven years. "And I'm certain that in a few years we'll have to revamp them again. But for now I'm comfortable we've done what we have to do to meet our goals. If one of us dies, the other inherits the other's whole estate and, of course, would be responsible for taking care of our child. Dick also has a $50,000 insurance policy naming the children from his first marriage as beneficiaries.

"We had the most difficult time figuring out what to do if

we died simultaneously — or almost simultaneously. Here's what we decided. All that we own jointly — and that's just about everything of value, like our home, cars, and some shares in mutual funds — will be split in half. Dick's estate will be divided in three equal shares to reflect his fathering of three children. Mine will remain intact for our son who will need more money for a longer period of time than Dick's children, who are already in their teens. We've named my sister as our son's guardian.

"But there's more," Samantha explains. "Dividing the property that way in our wills left me emotionally uneasy because Dick's daughter has been living with us for the past three years and I've grown very close to her. I want to leave her something just from me. So I opened up a bank account in trust for her, to which I add small sums from time to time."

Dick and Samantha stripped together four parts to come out with a viable estate plan: wills, bank accounts, joint tenancy, and insurance.

One entrepreneur and his assets. Perry has substantially more money than Linda, primarily because he has a successful dry cleaning store in the Seattle vicinity. His son from his first marriage had just entered the business when he and Linda were wed four years ago. With the exception of a $50,000 CD and the condo he and Linda bought together, all of his money was tied up in the business. Perry had two concerns when he redrafted his will: making certain Linda was well provided for in case of his death (she has no living parents and no children) and leaving the business to his son. Working with his attorney and insurance broker, he entered into a buy-sell agreement that would assure the sale of the business to his son when he died. The son would fund the agreement by buying life insurance on his father's life so he could pay the estate (which was left to Linda) the fixed buyout price. Each year Perry makes a cash gift to his son to cover the cost of the insurance premium. This estate plan assures him that the business will go to his son and that Linda will have a large pool of liquid assets.

Money versus things: How to even it out. One would think that as cofounders of the Stepfamily Association, authors of three books on stepfamilies, and a couple who have been married over 30 years, John and Emily Visher would be able to reach easy decisions when it came to who gets what. Not so. They, too, had to do some creative thinking in the past few years when they discovered a problem with their estate plan. After putting "her stuff," "his stuff," and "their stuff" on three imaginary tables, "her stuff" consisted of valuable family heirlooms, while his table looked pretty bare. They pondered about how they were going to even things out.

"After speaking to the children [adults], we came up with this solution," John says. "We're going to try to balance out the inequity in our wills by leaving the children different amounts of cash. Hopefully, Emily's four children and my three will feel they have been treated fairly."

Times for Revisions

Just as the process of bringing up children needs midcourse corrections from time to time, estate planning is a process that needs updating or periodic revising. Samantha is right. Her estate plan will need to be reviewed again. The trigger times for revision are when

1. Your circumstances change considerably. Once your estate exceeds $600,000, you need careful financial planning because of onerous estate taxes. Figure estate taxes will be 50% on amounts over $600,000 if left to anyone (or any group of people) other than your spouse. Anything you can do to reduce that tax will leave more money to your beneficiaries and less to the government.

2. You or one of your beneficiaries develops a serious

health problem, perhaps an ongoing one that will drain the family of money.

3. You have children — or more children. You need to take their needs into consideration.

4. You want to change the personal guardian you have named for your children.

5. An heir marries, has children, dies, or becomes estranged.

6. Tax laws affecting estates shift.

7. You divorce.

8. You move to a different state. (This is especially necessary if you move from a common law property state to a community property state or vice versa.)

Keeping Track of Where Everything Is

Now that you've put your estate in order it's time to do the same with your papers.

Most people keep important papers and possessions in different places — safe-deposit box, file cabinets, home safes, desk drawers, even dresser drawers. It's hard enough for us to remember where we put something a year ago; think of how hard it would be if heirs had to go on a document hunt after you died. It might be years before they could find all the important information.

Use the "Paper Trail" worksheet to keep track of your estate planning documents as well as your important financial records. Then make three copies of it. Send one to the executor of your estate, one to a beneficiary, and keep the third in a desk drawer.

"PAPER TRAIL" Worksheet

For: _____ and _____ .

Social Security #s _____ and _____ .

Legend:

   1 = Safe-deposit box _____ at _____
                     (number)   (bank and address)

   2 = Home safe

   3 = Office safe

   4 = Lawyer's _____ office at _____
                (name)   (address)

   5 = Metal box at home in the _____
                            (location)

   6 = Desk at home or in office

   7 = At bank _____
              (name of bank / person to contact / address)

   8 = At brokerage _____
               (name of firm / person to contact / address)

   9 = Other _____

Use the legend
to indicate the
location for   Item

Husband	Wife	
_____	_____	Original will
_____	_____	Copy of will
_____	_____	Living will documents
_____	_____	Letters of last instructions
_____	_____	Personal letters to be distributed after death
_____	_____	Trust agreements
_____	_____	Life insurance policies
_____	_____	Health insurance policies
_____	_____	Property and casualty policies
_____	_____	Annuity contracts
_____	_____	Car insurance policies

_____	_____	Deed to automobile
_____	_____	Deed to home
_____	_____	Safe combinations
_____	_____	Bank records
_____	_____	Checkbook
_____	_____	Savings and loan records and accounts
_____	_____	Tax records
_____	_____	Record of debts owed to and owed by you
_____	_____	Employment contracts
_____	_____	Corporate retirement plans
_____	_____	Stock option plans
_____	_____	Keogh or IRA plans
_____	_____	Partnership agreements
_____	_____	List of credit cards
_____	_____	Stock, bond, and brokerage records (including certificates)
_____	_____	Mutual fund record
_____	_____	Other real estate deeds
_____	_____	Other investments
_____	_____	Powers of attorney
_____	_____	Cemetery plot deed
_____	_____	Other
_____	_____	_____
_____	_____	_____

Congratulations. You've cleared the hardest psychological hurdle of the financial planning process — estate planning. Having successfully grappled with some of the most complex and emotional questions, you should be able to face other financial challenges with the confidence of an Olympian.

Chapter 11

With This Checklist, I Thee Wed

THE FINANCIAL ACTION PLAN

[ ] Establish a joint bank account
[ ] Rent a safe-deposit box in a joint name
[ ] Update your W-4 form to reflect the new number of dependents
[ ] If there's a name or address change, notify Social Security, the IRS, the motor vehicle bureau, credit card companies, employers
[ ] Rethink your tax situation and make necessary adjustments
[ ] Review insurance coverage — life, disability, car, home
[ ] Change beneficiary designations on life insurance, pension or profit-sharing plans, bank accounts
[ ] Coordinate medical and hospital benefits
[ ] Reevaluate investments
[ ] Sift through financial files

This is an exciting time — the beginning of life as a married couple. Together you will set a financial course for yourselves that will serve as the direction for years to come. Some of the turns are sharper on this course because of the complexity of remarriage; some are easily negotiable because you've been around them before. Buying your new bed, renting a safe-deposit box, or working out a preliminary financial plan for two are ground-breaking and, yes, romantic activities.

Many of the financial actions taken as a couple are evolutionary ones, like deciding on a comprehensive estate plan. But the ones in the checklist beginning this chapter are not. To keep you on a straight financial course, they should be done either right before or right after remarriage.

Designate an "Our" Bank

Assuming you're going to have a joint account, set it up at a bank that's convenient to both of you (this doesn't preclude each of you from having your own account elsewhere). This "household" account gives each of you easy access to depositing and withdrawing money. Rent a joint safe-deposit box at this bank as well, into which you transfer all your important papers (separation and divorce decrees, marriage and birth certificates, stock certificates, titles to cars, homes, et cetera).

Formulate a provisional plan for (1) who's going to be responsible for bill paying from the account; (2) a financial record-keeping system (for example, you may choose to keep a running total in a checking account or to tally the figures at the end of each month); (3) what will be paid for out of the joint account; and (4) how much each partner can withdraw without discussing it with the other.

Taxes for Two

Wedding time. If you have the choice between getting married in December or January, factor in taxes before you decide.

If one of you has considerably less income than the other, opt for December. You will generally be taxed less if you are married and filing jointly than you would be if each of you filed separate returns.

If both of you have similar levels of income, choose January. There's a glitch in the tax code that penalizes married couples who earn approximately the same income. They usually pay more tax than if they filed two single returns.

Dependency exemption. Child custody arrangements affect taxes. Here's how it works. The parent who has custody of a child for the greater part of the year claims the exemption, no matter how little he or she contributes toward the child's financial support. (This practice continues through college. The child can be claimed as a dependent if your home continues to be his or her primary residence.) If, as a result of your remarriage, your child comes to live with you and your new spouse for most of the year, you can take the dependency exemption on your tax return — even if your separation agreement says something else. The only way the IRS recognizes a different arrangement is if you sign a form waiving your right to this exemption and your former spouse attaches it to his or her return. (Be certain only one parent claims the exemption. You'll wind up owing additional taxes and penalties if the deduction is disallowed.)

Moving deduction. A surprise tax deduction might be available to people who move and change jobs as a result of the remarriage. Moving expenses incurred as a result of switching jobs, if the location of your new job is at least 35 miles farther from your residence than your old job was, are often tax deductible — assuming you find another job rather quickly.

Here's the employment test. If you're an employee, you must be working full-time at your new job location for at least 39 weeks of the 12-month period that follows your move to the new location.

If you're self-employed, there's an additional requirement. You must work full-time, as either an employee or self-employed person, at your new job location for at least 78 weeks of the 24-month period following your move.

The employment requirement obviously is waived in the event of your death or disability. It's also waived if you're fired, laid off, or transferred for reasons other than willful misconduct.

Tax-deductible IRA. Even if you are eligible for a tax-deductible IRA (an account that lets you set aside up to $2,000 a year for your retirement using pretax dollars) and you've been doing it for years, if your new spouse isn't eligible, you are no longer either.

Once you're married, if you and your spouse file jointly, the only way you can continue to claim an IRA deduction on your tax return is if neither of you are an active participant in a qualified retirement plan or if jointly your adjusted gross income doesn't exceed $50,000.

Inequity of tax payments. Discuss how you're going to handle tax payments when you're married and filing jointly. This becomes a consideration especially when one spouse is earning considerably more than the other. Ellen and Kurt are a good example of the problem. Ellen earns $25,000 a year. When she was single she filed as a head of household and was in the 15% tax bracket. Kurt earns $90,000 and is in the highest tax bracket. Now that they're married they're filing a joint return. Ellen knows she can't afford to split the tax indebtedness with Kurt; Kurt doesn't expect it.

They've looked at two possibilities. The simplest would be to apply the ratio of their income to their share of the taxes. That means Ellen would contribute about 22%, Kurt 78%.

But the income tax system is progressive, so a simple proportion may not be equitable. Another arrangement, fairer in absolute terms, is that Ellen would not pay more taxes married than she would have paid if she were filing as she had before as a head of household.

Additional Responsibility, Additional Insurance

Step over the threshold of your new remarriage and tumbling in with you are more kids, more cars, more pets, more family and friends.

Financial translation: more or different insurance.

Homeowner's insurance. If one of you is moving into another's home, the additional furniture, electronic equipment, and "stuff" means you need more homeowner's coverage because the policy covers the home *and* its contents. Grab a notebook. You'll have to do a personal property inventory to determine the amount of coverage needed. (The inventory also helps you settle a claim if a loss occurs.) You might want to add a personal property floater policy to extend protection to expensive personal items, such as heirloom jewelry, that are otherwise slighted in a standard homeowner's policy.

Renters, too, need property insurance. Landlords are held liable for losses to your property only if you can prove they were negligent — as in not providing the doorman security that they said they would.

Liability coverage. With more people traipsing in and out of the house, there's an increased chance of an accident in which someone is hurt. So consider increasing the liability portion of your homeowner's insurance or, if you think you're a prime target for large liability claims because your combined incomes are substantial, purchase an umbrella policy that provides liability coverage of one million dollars or more for homeowner's and automobile insurance.

Life insurance. Do you need additional life insurance to protect your new spouse? Probably. If your divorce agreement mandates that you keep a policy with a former spouse as beneficiary, you must abide by that. It doesn't work to change the beneficiary designation on that policy to your new spouse. When you die, your former spouse could sue and collect under the terms of the divorce or separation agreement, leaving your spouse hefty legal bills but no insurance.

Disability insurance. Few remarried couples can afford the loss of one income for any significant period, so if you aren't already covered, waste no time in getting disability insurance. At the age of 35, the chance of becoming seriously disabled for three months or more is nearly three times as great as the chance of dying. At 50, the odds are nearly four times greater. Social Security disability insurance is helpful only in the most extreme cases; even then you must expect to be out of work for a year and not able to do *any* significant work. Some large companies provide employees with disability insurance; most do not. So you may be forced to get private insurance, which will replace 60 to 70% of your income. Look for policies that (1) allow you to boost your coverage if your income increases; (2) can't be canceled as long as you pay your premium; (3) will provide coverage if you can't do the type of work you're used to doing — not just if you can't do any work; (4) will allow you to ease back into work without losing all your benefits; and (5) have automatic cost-of-living increases. To shave premiums, stretch the elimination period, the time between when income stops and benefits begin, for as long as your personal resources will allow.

Automobile insurance. Car insurance probably will need updating. In some cases there might be a savings. The insurance on three cars registered at one address usually costs less than the sum of the premiums on two cars insured in one household and one car in another. On the other hand, if your new spouse comes with a daredevil teenage driver, rates will skyrocket.

Change Beneficiaries

Life insurance policies often need to have the beneficiary changed. You probably will remember to do that for the policy you own individually, but don't forget the group policy taken out by your company. That, too, needs to be reviewed.

Change the beneficiary designations on your pensions, Keogh accounts, and IRAs. A former spouse may still have rights to a retirement account during the first year of a remarriage unless you change the beneficiary.

Merge Benefits

Working husbands and wives come to this marriage toting two separate benefits packages. What better time than right now to weed out duplicate coverage and maximize benefits.

• If each of you is covered under a group insurance plan that covers 80% of your medical expenses, you should consider adding each other and all the dependent children to both plans. After you file with your insurance company and your claim is reimbursed (up to 80%), your spouse files with his or hers to collect the remaining 20%. Your plans work together to provide up to 100% of your covered expenses. Generally, this works well for families of four or more. If yours is a small, exceptionally healthy family, it may not be worth the additional premium for complete coverage. In that case, enroll the children in the plan with the better benefits.

• Which of you has employers matching contributions to 401(k) plans? If one has none and the other has employers contributing 50% of what you or your spouse contribute, there's no doubt about which plan should receive most of your retirement funds. The person without matching funds should stop contributing to the plan, thereby increasing his or her take-home pay. If the spouse who continues contributing increases the amount, the couple comes out ahead.

• Consider the immediate needs of the new marriage and don't stash away money you're going to need now. If you wind up withdrawing money meant for retirement (in IRAs, Keoghs, 401(k), or pension plans) earlier than age 59½, you'll pay a 10% penalty and the IRS will count the funds as taxable income in the year they're withdrawn.

• If you have a flexible benefit plan at work, one that allows you a choice of benefits, coordinate coverage with your spouse. You might be able to trade vacation days for money or vice versa — depending on what the family needs at the moment. Be wary about dropping medical coverage, however, especially if your spouse's job isn't deadbolt secure. You could run into problems. Few, if any, companies will reinstate medical coverage, life insurance, or long-term disability benefits without proof of good health. And if you want to reinstate dental insurance, you may be asked to wait a year.

Review Investments

Whether you plan to merge your investments or maintain separate portfolios, give your investments the once-over early in your marriage so that you can begin to create a workable, diversified, intelligent "family" package — one you both understand and could handle in case of an emergency where one of you has to take over management for the other.

The investments people bring to a remarriage may not be as colorful as their plaid armchairs and scarlet sofas, but they "fit" their owners just as well. As there is no perfect chair, so there is no "right" investment. Right depends upon who you are — your age, occupation, number of dependents, health, investment knowledge, insurance coverage, net worth, *and* your ability to feel at ease with your holdings (your "risk comfort level"). Suppose one of you has a vast knowledge of the economy and investment markets. At any given time, that spouse may own shares in growth and single-country mutual funds and have gold coins in the vault. The less sophisticated of you may be glued to two investments: bank CDs and Treasury notes. Who's going to make more money over a given period of time? The 1990s failures of the 1980s financial gurus just prove the suspicions of the wise cynics: nobody knows. "Even when the experts all agree, they may well be mistaken," philosopher Bertrand Russell said. Individually, neither the sophisticated risk taker nor the conservative, risk-averse investor in this example has a solidly diversified portfolio; coupled, however, the extreme positions provide ballast for one another.

Risk wisely. Remarriage is risky. Yet you're not going to give up this relationship because the risk is great. By reading this book, you're decreasing the risk that your remarriage will fail. You're arming yourself with knowledge and strategies for meeting its challenges and successfully negotiating them.

Investing is risky. But just as remarriage can be richly rewarding, so investing can be — as long as it's carefully thought out. Taking too much risk is misguided; so is taking too little. Ditch the idea that there is a perfectly risk-free investment. Although it will provide you with a rate of return that seems fair when you buy it, even the honorable Treasury bond can be a loser if you're locked into it at an annual interest rate of 5% during a time when the inflation rate is a soaring 12%.

There is a tenet in investing that can be applied to marriage: the greater the possible return, the higher the risk.

Investment guidelines. How do you cut the rate of failure when risking money? What's a prudent, thought-out risk?

1. *Look for an investment that has a high probability of return* (nothing is guaranteed), one that doesn't have an all-or-

nothing bottom line, and one that gives you opportunity to sell it at a later date (if that's what you choose to do).

2. *Balance your portfolio* so that you have diversity and liquidity (money available for almost-instant use) between you.

3. *Set simple plans in motion that will keep your investments growing.* The early years of remarriage are often chaotic. For those who don't have long stretches of time to develop investment strategies, or for those who aren't interested in studying investments, consider some painless, almost automatic ways to keep accumulating investment dollars.

- An automatic payroll deduction plan where your employer deducts a set amount from your paycheck and transfers it to a money market account or savings plan. If your company doesn't have such a plan, banks do. With your authorization they'll subtract a stipulated amount from your checking account on a predetermined date and transfer the money into a money market account.

- Reinvesting the dividends you receive as a shareholder in a public company or mutual fund, or as a bondholder. Check the company's literature for how to set the reinvestment process in motion automatically.

- An installment-plan technique called dollar-cost averaging. Each month you invest a set amount in, for example, a particular mutual fund. The amount is always the same whether the price of the shares is up or down. Over time, you're likely to accumulate more shares at a median price than at high prices. For example, one month $100 will buy 10 shares of a mutual fund selling at $10 per share, and the next month it will buy about 14 shares at

$7.15 a share. You wind up with 24 shares at an average price of $8.33 under dollar-cost averaging.

Sort, Save, and Dump Financial Records

Best if you can sift through financial records *before* remarriage so you don't pay movers to cart files you're going to wind up throwing out. Here's what to keep and what to toss.

Income tax records. In general, the IRS has three years from the date your tax return is due to challenge it. So keep your '88 return (filed in April 1989) until April 1992; your '89 return (filed in April 1990) until April 1993, and so on.

But . . . audit time limits are extended to six years if the IRS can show that you failed to report income exceeding 25% of what you reported. If there's any possibility of that, '88 returns filed in April 1989 should be held until April 1995; '89 returns filed in April 1990 should be held until April 1996, et cetera.

All bets are off if fraud is involved. There's no statute of limitations then.

Keep your tax records

3 years — if your income consists only of interest earnings and wages reported on a W-2
6 years — if you're an independent contractor reporting business income on Schedule C
Forever — if there could be any doubt about the veracity of your return

Home records. Save all the receipts for home improvements and repairs such as the purchase of a new boiler, patio or bathroom renovations, the installation of central air conditioning, or building of a new wing. Anything that can be added to your home's purchase price to increase its cost basis and reduce your capital gain will help you minimize taxes when you sell.

If you've sold a home and reported the sale on Tax Form 2119, generally all you need to keep are the settlement statements, Form 2119, and receipts for home improvements.

Keep the information on the latest assessment on your home. Keep the canceled checks for any property taxes paid.

Retirement accounts. Trash all but the most recent quarterly reports of transactions and annuity benefits reports. But keep — indefinitely — records pertaining to nondeductible IRA contributions, including Tax Form 8606.

Divorce decrees and death certificates. At least for the first few years of a remarriage, keep all the papers and letters from a former spouse that might be relevant in the event of any court proceedings. When animosities abate and your former spouse seems to have gotten on with his or her life, that's the time to toss them. Keep separation and divorce decrees forever, however. The same holds true for the death certificate of a former spouse.

Investments. The "toss" list:

• expired CDs (once you receive Tax Form 1099 and verify the interest earning reported)

• all but the most recent money market account statements and the one for the previous December (which gives you the tax information you'll need to file your return in April)

• annual reports of companies in which you own stock and shareholders reports on your mutual funds (once you've read them)

• all but the first and the last prospectuses from mutual funds you are invested in, and all but your latest cumulative report on transactions and the December year-end cumulative report

• the quarterly distribution statements of limited partnerships (but keep your original prospectus and K-1 tax forms)

The "keep" list:

• Confirmations of all purchases and redemptions of stocks and bonds for as long as you own them. When you sell, keep the papers for as long as you retain tax records. Also keep a record of dividends that have been reinvested.

• Tax Form 8583 for passive activity loss limitations. If you can't deduct passive losses, such as those from rental real estate, keep this form until the property is sold, when those losses can be claimed.

Bank records. Keep canceled checks and bank statements for as long as you keep tax returns. (Once you've checked deposit slips against the statements you can toss them, however.) The procedure changes with savings accounts. For these, you need keep only the latest statement and the one for the previous December.

Unless you use them as a backup for a tax deduction or a warranty, keep credit card monthly statements for only a year.

Automobiles. Keep the purchase order and title and confirmation of the car loan you paid off (just in case there's still a record of a lien on it when you sell the car). Also keep the car's maintenance records (so you can give them to the new owner when you sell it) and your most recent registration and insurance papers. Toss all other papers relating to the car.

Insurance. Scrap canceled or outdated policies — car, home, or life. Keep only current policies.

Hold on to only the most recent copies of annuity and cash value reports relating to life policies.

Information relating to car and home claims settled more than a year ago can be tossed.

Medical and dental insurance reimbursement statements should be kept for at least a year, and, if you're going to be taking a tax deduction for medical expenses, keep them (and the medical bills) for as long as you keep your tax records.

If you change jobs, keep the summary of medical coverage from your previous employer for a year to track coverage of preexisting conditions in case you have to settle old claims.

Odds and ends. Keep Tax Form 942, which records paying Social Security tax and federal unemployment insurance for household employees, just in case a former employee asserts, sometime in the future, that you didn't make the required contributions.

Toss — expired warranties, phone and utility bills over a year old (unless they are part of the home office deductions you're taking on a tax return), and all but your most recent and the previous December's pay stubs.

Remarriage presents a rare opportunity to start again, to right what was wrong with the financial arrangements of a former life, to turn chaos into order. Use the Financial Action Plan to make this an easy and enlightened time of financial transition.

Chapter 12

Conclusion

The American family is a remarried family. Call us blended, reconstituted, step. Whatever our designation, we're now the contemporary American family.

Picture these images of our financial woes. Don't they look mischievously close even when viewed from a safe distance?

• A husband and wife, seated at a dining-room table strewn with papers, bills, statements, and checkbooks, poring over a phone bill. They're clearly in a snit over whose children called Dallas and whose called Chicago.

• A man stuffing an oversize envelope marked "alimony" into a mailbox. He's glaring. His wife stands next to him; she's peeved (but it's hard to know if her anger is directed at her husband or the unknown recipient of the envelope).

• A harried husband and wife coming home from work being met by four children — two teenage boys obviously his, one teenage girl obviously hers, and a toddler who looks like both of them. One boy is grabbing for the keys to a car, another is holding up a piece of paper indicating how much his hockey uniform will cost. The girl is pointing to a picture of a computer with pleading eyes, and the toddler is crying because he doesn't want his baby-sitter to leave.

Narrowly focusing on the sometimes gloomy, confusing, or bizarre financial situations we find ourselves in, we can make the mistake of losing the background against which these remarital scenes are set. In a committed remarriage, the backdrop is one of adventure and love. A sense of humor serves as a telephoto lens; it helps isolate a ridiculous, hilarious, or ludicrous moment. Increasing exposure by taking more time to view the scene is the major ally in lightening up the picture.

I now have the time to look back on how we handled our finances in the first, say, seven years of our remarriage. Let me share with you some of what we did wrong.

• I like resolution. So every time we closed our bedroom door to "discuss" my anxiety about our precarious financial position, I expected we'd emerge two hours later with a solution in hand. My expectations were unreal.

• I assumed too many of the financial chores. In my first marriage I had abdicated almost all of the financial responsibilities. When I divorced, I felt I'd been scalded because of my financial nincompoopery. In my "never again" mode, I mistook scut work for power.

• We didn't do a "Budgetview" until years after we were married. The whole idea of accounting for every expenditure was abhorrent to both of us. Neither could we stand thinking of ourselves as detail people. While my husband felt comfortable enough with his mental math, I didn't. I wallowed in worry without knowing if there was reason for it.

We're not through with our financial work yet. In addition to the evolutionary and ongoing future decisions we'll have to make, we still haven't done some of what we should have.

We haven't filled out the "Paper Trail" worksheet and given copies of it to one, two, or all of the children.

We haven't signed living wills, though they're sitting on the desk.

We haven't thrown away the yellowing tax records of the 1970s and early 1980s cluttering the closet shelves.

I don't consider these grievous problems. They'll get done. Sometime.

It's what we've done right, after some bumbling starts, that will in the long run best serve our marriage. And we're not alone. The underlying threads that ran through the stories of every successfully remarried couple I interviewed for this book were the same.

We are tenacious about problem solving. If one "solution" proves elusive, we try another. The pieces to the puzzle are all there, we reason. Our job is to keep trying to put it together.

We communicate and compromise. So much time was spent talking, listening, and yes, screaming about financial differences early on, that eventually we learned to hear each other.

From the beginning, we subscribed to the philosophy of "what's important to you is important to me." That doesn't mean agreeing. It means respecting differences.

We have been determined to make the marriage work because we care deeply about one another.

Like the ingredients in Grandma's special cake, the ingredients for financial compatibility can't be measured. Each couple creates its own personal blend depending upon such standard financial factors as priorities, needs, obligations, goals, the amount of money available. The spices — whether you're a free spender or freeloader, a complainer or a coper, or whether your money motivation is for power, love, security, or freedom — will add flavor and interest to your financial future as a couple.

For my husband and me, it has been 15 years and counting. Our understanding of how to manage a financial union has evolved over that time.

We have made it clear to each other what we *can't* live

with and have been discovering what we *want* to live with, what we *enjoy* living with. He still thinks it's overkill to traipse to nine different dealerships in four counties over a period of three weekends just to negotiate a $500 price break on a car. I have a nagging feeling it's important. But I don't chastise him as a careless spender, nor does he castigate me with taunts of "cheapskate." We just have different styles and have learned to compromise. Last time we bought a new car it meant two weekends, two dealers, and $1,400 off list price. We walked away hand in hand and pleased with ourselves — even though we'll never know if we had the best deal in four counties.

Though nobody denies it's better to have enough money than to brood about how you're going to earn the next dollar or spend every cent, wealth doesn't necessarily pave the way for a rich remarriage. Kristine, a buyer at a major department store in San Francisco when she married Charlie eight years ago, described what has made her marriage so rich.

"I knew Charlie was dedicated to upholding the major financial commitment he had to his first wife and two children," she says. "And I suspected that he wouldn't be able to contribute much to our household initially because at the time he was only a moderately recognized artist with a fluctuating income. But since I was well paid, we didn't feel the pinch.

"Then I became pregnant," Kristine says. "When I was in my sixth month, Charlie was offered a job in the art department of a major movie studio. The salary was spectacular and would have put us in another ballpark. Charlie wavered. He hated the idea of reporting to someone who would criticize his work based on commercial standards, but he knew I wanted to be home with the baby and he didn't want me to worry about our finances. 'We're going to have a baby. I have to consider it,' he said. We agonized over the offer because, in reality, I was worried about money. I could see that as much as he wanted to provide me with peace of mind, this job would stifle him. When I finally said 'I think this is wrong

for you and I don't want you to take it just for me,' he was visibly
moved . . . and relieved."

That was three years and two babies ago. Kristine hasn't
gone back to retailing yet. "At first, I resented his former wife
because of the money she was getting for child support. Then
I wondered about the wisdom of Charlie's job decision because we had to cut back on our spending considerably," she
continues. "But I don't wonder anymore. Having children
myself makes me more empathetic to his former wife's needs.
As for Charlie's work, I'm thrilled. If I had to face a resentful
man every night, we wouldn't be married. Instead, when
Charlie comes home from the studio, I am greeted by a ful-
filled person who shows me in many different ways how
thankful he is that I didn't pressure him into a nine-to-five
job."

An exciting aspect of remarriage is that personally and as
a couple you have a rare opportunity to redefine your financial goals. Though the definition of what makes a financially
successful couple is personal and subjective, the path to
achieving harmony is simple — at times, easier to read about
than to follow. It rests on two principles: this relationship is
worth having, and this relationship is worth working for.
Over the years you build on that, learning to communicate
your financial feelings and needs, respecting each other's
differences, compromising when appropriate, and behaving
as financial equals.

These are the investments in the remarriage. With each,
financial unity compounds. Per annum, the financial relationship swells with a wealth that is one part money, one
part trust, one part love.

Bibliography

BOOKS

Barsness, Anita O. *Money Matters in Second Marriages*. Milwaukee: Center for Consumer Affairs, University of Wisconsin, 1986.

Berman, Claire. *Making It As a Stepparent: New Roles — New Rules*. New York: Perennial Library, 1986.

Bernstein, Anne C. *Yours, Mine, and Ours: How Families Change When Remarried Parents Have a Child Together*. New York: W. W. Norton & Company, Inc., 1990.

Bernstein, Peter W., ed. *Ernst & Young's Tax-Saving Strategies 1990–1991*. New York: John Wiley & Sons, Inc., 1990.

Blumstein, Philip, and Pepper Schwartz. *American Couples*. New York: Pocket Books, 1985.

Clifford, Denis. *Plan Your Estate: Wills, Probate Avoidance, Trusts and Taxes*. Berkeley, Calif.: Nolo Press, 1989.

Dunn, Dick. *Preparing to Marry Again*. Roswell, Ga.: Singles Ministry Resources, 1988.

Edelstein, Scott. *Putting Your Kids Through College*. Mount Vernon, N.Y.: Consumer Reports Books, 1989.

Einstein, Elizabeth. *The Stepfamily: Living, Loving, and Learning*. New York: Shambhala, 1985.

Felton-Collins, Victoria. *Couples and Money: Why Money Interferes with Love and What to Do About It*. New York: Bantam Books, 1990.

Fisher, Roger, and William Ury. *Getting to Yes: Negotiating Agreement Without Giving In*. New York: Penguin, 1983.

Gitman, Lawrence J., and Michael D. Joehnk. *Personal Financial Planning*. Chicago: The Dryden Press, 1990.

Ihara, Toni, and Ralph Warner. *The Living Together Kit*. Berkeley, Calif.: Nolo Press, 1990.

Klagsbrun, Francine. *Married People: Staying Together in the Age of Divorce.* New York: Bantam Books, 1985.

Lowe, Patricia. *The Cruel Stepmother.* Englewood Cliffs, N.J.: Prentice Hall, 1970.

Matthews, Joseph L., and Dorothy M. Berman. *Social Security, Medicare and Pensions.* Berkeley, Calif.: Nolo Press, 1990.

Pasley, Kay, and Marilyn Ihinger-Tallman, eds. *Remarriage and Stepparenting: Current Research and Theory.* New York: Guilford Press, 1987.

Plesent, Stanley. *Preparing Matrimonial Agreements.* New York: Practising Law Institute, 1989.

Sabo, Marcella M., Rosana Gershman, and Geraldine Lee Waxman. *Whose Kid Is It Anyway? and Over Four Hundred Other Questions for Divorcing, Dating and Remarried Families.* Astoria, Oreg.: NextStep Publications, 1989.

Stepfamily Association of America, Inc. *The Stepping Ahead Program.* Baltimore: Stepfamily Association of America, Inc., 1988.

Strauss, Peter J., Robert Wolf, and Dana Shilling. *Aging and the Law.* Chicago: Commerce Clearing House, 1990.

Westoff, Leslie Aldridge. *The Second Time Around.* New York: The Viking Press, 1977.

Yalom, Irvin D. *Love's Executioner.* New York: Basic Books, Inc., 1989.

ARTICLES AND PAMPHLETS

Angier, Natalie. "Marriage Is a Lifesaver for Men After 45." *New York Times,* October 16, 1990.

Brooks, Andree. "Can't Sell? A Tenant Could Help." *New York Times,* September 30, 1990.

Coleman, Marilyn, and Lawrence Ganong. "An Evaluation of the Stepfamily Self-Help Literature." *Family Relations,* January 1987.

——— "Financial Decisions Shared In Remarriages." *Stepfamily Bulletin,* Summer 1989.

——— "Remarriage and Stepfamily Research in the 1980s." *Journal of Marriage and the Family,* November 1990.

Estess, Patricia Schiff. "The Stepfamily Finances Puzzle." *Sylvia Porter's Personal Finance,* March 1989.

——— "Should You Lend Money to a Relative?" *Parade,* July 24, 1988.

Green, Laura. "How to Make the Significant Choices." *Lear's,* June 1990.

Ihinger-Tallman, Marilyn, and Kay Pasley. "Remarriage and Integration Within the Community." *Journal of Marriage and the Family*, May 1986.

Kantrowitz, Barbara, and Pat Wingert. "Step by Step." *Newsweek* Special Issue, 1990.

Kutner, Lawrence. "The Concerns of Adults When a Parent Remarries." *New York Times*, November 30, 1989.

——— "To Avoid the Bitterness and Pain of Fights Over Wills." *New York Times*, May 17, 1990.

Luciano, Lani. "Homestuck." *Money*, January 1990.

Malone, Thomas P. "Modification Lives." *Family Advocate*, Spring 1988.

Metzen, Anita, and Edward Metzen. "Stages in Money Management for Stepfamilies." *Stepfamily Bulletin*, Fall 1988.

Miller, Louisa F., and Jeanne E. Moorman. "Married-Couple Families with Children." *Studies in Marriage and the Family*, Bureau of the Census, September 1989.

Papernow, Patricia L. "Thickening the 'Middle Ground.' " *Psychotherapy*, Fall 1987.

——— "The Stepfamily Cycle." *Family Relations*, July 1984.

Peers, Alexandra. "Who Gets the Kids?" *Wall Street Journal*, May 15, 1987.

Rock, Andrea. "Can You Afford Your Kids?" *Money*, July 1990.

Rowland, Mary. "Linking Love and Money." *New York Times*, February 2, 1990.

Solomon, Carmen D. "The Family Support Act of 1988." *CRS Report for Congress*, November 7, 1988.

Stepfamily Foundation. "The Dynamics of Step," n.d.